Praise

Women Run the World
Sh*t Gets Done

"This is a book about what is possible. It's about community and courage. This is a book about what it means to speak out against violence, injustice, and apathy. This is a book about the power women have—and are using to help heal the broken bones of this beautiful world. For too long, women's voices have been overshadowed. This is a book of stories that will light you up with hope. After you read it, you'll be inspired to use your own voice in a new way. I promise."

—Sherry Richert Belul, author of *Say it Now: 33 Creative Ways to Say I Love You to the Most Important People in Your Life*

"Honest, thoughtful, and enlightening, When Women Run the World *is about representation—who has it, who needs it, and who deserves more of it. This glorious book engages our sensibilities and intellects, and compels the reader without letting us merely settle into its pages as entertainment. After reading Rachanow, I felt illuminated. Charged. Shelly Rachanow's creative activist and feminist voice deserves a wide audience."*

—M. J. Fievre, author of *A Sky the Color of Chaos* and *Badass Black Girl*

When Women Run the World Sh*t Gets Done

Also by
Shelly Rachanow

If Women Ran the World, Sh*t Would Get Done

What Would You Do If YOU Ran the World?

When Women Run the World Sh*t Gets Done

Celebrating the Power of Women Now

Shelly Rachanow

Conari
Press

CORAL GABLES

Cover Design: Roberto Nunez

Interior Layout Design: Jermaine Lau

Published by Conari Press, an imprint of Mango Media Inc.

For permission requests, please contact the publisher at:

Mango Publishing Group
2850 Douglas Road, 2nd Floor
Coral Gables, FL 33134 USA
info@mango.bz

For special orders, quantity sales, course adoptions and corporate sales, please email the publisher at sales@mango.bz. For trade and wholesale sales, please contact Ingram Publisher Services at customer.service@ingramcontent.com or +1.800.509.4887.

When Women Run the World Sh*t Gets Done: Celebrating the Power of Women Now

ISBN: (p) 978-1-64250-393-7 (e) 978-1-64250-394-4

BISAC: POL052000, POLITICAL SCIENCE / Women in Politics

LCCN: 2020940960

To all women—past, present, and future—who work to make the world a better place and improve the lives of people everywhere. Thank you.

"I'M ABSOLUTELY
CONFIDENT THAT, FOR TWO
YEARS, IF EVERY NATION
ON EARTH WAS RUN BY
WOMEN, YOU WOULD SEE A
SIGNIFICANT IMPROVEMENT
ACROSS THE BOARD ON
JUST ABOUT EVERYTHING...
LIVING STANDARDS
AND OUTCOMES."

—US President Barack Obama

Table of Contents

Introduction

A chorus of women's voices grows around the world. And with each new voice the chorus grows louder, the chorus grows stronger, until it becomes deafening. The time to be silent is over.

In recent years, women have marched, taken to social media and raised our voices for equality and rights, pussy hats and all. We have taken on governments and fought against the towers of inequality and injustice. We have had the courage to say #MeToo and bring predators to their knees, letting their names be known.

Around the world, we have fought to end childhood marriage and gain equal inheritance laws. In many places, young girls are risking their lives for an education and dreaming of a job, let alone a career.

In fact, record numbers of us have run for office, so we can have a greater say about our rights and our bodies. Millions have protested against climate change, for LGBTQ rights, marriage equality, equal pay—and, above all, against the self-professed "pussy grabber" winning the US presidency.

We have done all these deeds in the name of accountability and decency, to honor and protect our rights and the rights of our future generations, to never fail in our commitment to ensure safety and respect for each other no matter the moment...no matter the time.

This is our collective voice. This is our power. This is the power of women. And our stories are reverberating around the world.

Sometimes a woman's story starts with courage, like Sampat Pal Devi from Northern India, who one day saw a man beating his wife. When she begged him to stop, he beat her as well. The next day, she returned with a bamboo stick and five other women and they gave him the lashing he deserved. News of her actions quickly spread and soon dozens of women flocked to her, asking for help, while even more women joined her team—and now they are thousands of women strong. Known for their pink saris, chosen to "signify the womanhood and understated strength," the Gulabi Gang and its thousands of women have worked to stop child marriages, train women in self-defense, oppose corruption, publicly shame molesters, and encourage women to become financially independent. As they say on their website, "What cannot be endured must be cured."[1]

Sampat Pal Devi couldn't allow what she was seeing to continue, not just in that one moment, but within her community at large. And, by showing great courage, she started a movement.

Our stories are sometimes so big that they affect us globally. When a determined young woman learned about the devastating impact of climate change, she started skipping school and sitting outside the Swedish Parliament in August 2018 holding a sign that read *Skolstrejk för klimatet*: "School Strike for Climate."

Gradually, she was joined by a handful of people, then hundreds, then thousands, and within a month enough people had joined her protest that she decided they would strike every Friday until Sweden ratified the Paris Agreement. Across Europe, thousands of students began skipping school to protest inaction in their own countries, and by the end of 2018 they numbered tens of thousands strong. Then on September 20, 2019, four million people joined a global climate strike, the largest climate demonstration in history.[2]

In just thirteen months, one determined voice had become four million—and that number continues to grow.

While the leaders of some of the most powerful countries on the planet continue to deny the science and the evidence, Greta Thunberg refused to go back to school until people took notice...and began to take action. Named *TIME Magazine's* person of the year in 2019, she was the youngest person ever to receive the honor, at just sixteen.[3]

It is hard to ignore a voice of reason. It is harder to ignore a movement.

This is the power of women.

Together, we have the power to create a world where *all* women have equal rights, pay, respect, opportunity, and safety. A world where women aren't called "nasty" because their words are powerful or honest. A world filled with fundamental respect for people of all faiths, races, creeds, and orientations. There is so much more that unites us than divides us.

This is the world that millions of women have stood up for and marched in solidarity as one voice that no longer whispers but roars.

I've written this book to celebrate the power of women, to celebrate all that we've done in recent years. Because when women run the world—when we speak up and speak out—amazing sh*t gets done.

Throughout this book, you will find stories of extraordinary women who are speaking out for change at this pivotal time. You'll read about leaders, trailblazers, and activists. You'll read about a woman who ran for office to provide a better role model for her sons. A woman who started a nonprofit to help at-risk girls improve their self-esteem and honor forgotten women from history. A trauma surgeon who had the courage to stand up to the National Rifle Association when they told her to "stay in her lane." And a group of female firefighters from the United Kingdom training to trek an 1,180-mile (1,900-kilometer) stretch of the Antarctic to raise money for charities, shine a light on mental health, and show young girls that women are both strong and powerful, and can succeed in any profession they want.

Why these stories and why these women? Because, like you and like me, they saw a need and thought, "I can do something about this." Within each of us lies the strength and courage to make a difference in this world. It's my hope that these stories inspire and ignite a spark within you to contribute in whatever way you can and join the chorus of women's rights around our world.

Remember, one small action from each of us can inspire a movement. And as we've seen in recent years, movements can change minds—and ultimately, the world.

It is time to tell your story.

> "There is no greater agony than bearing an untold story inside you."
>
> —MAYA ANGELOU

#WomenGetShitDone #SpeakUpSpeakOut #NoLongerSilent

"I AM NO LONGER
ACCEPTING THE THINGS
I CANNOT CHANGE. I'M
CHANGING THE THINGS I
CANNOT ACCEPT."

—Angela Davis

Chapter One

Dr. Stephanie Bonne: #ThisIsOurLane

April 20, 1999. Columbine High School, Littleton, Colorado. Thirteen people murdered.

July 8, 2003. Lockheed Martin plant, Meridian, Mississippi. Six people murdered.

March 21, 2005. Red Lake High School and reservation, Red Lake, Minnesota. Nine people murdered.

April 16, 2007. Virginia Tech University, Blacksburg, Virginia. Thirty-two people murdered.

July 20, 2012. Aurora, Colorado, movie theater. Twelve people murdered.

December 14, 2012. Sandy Hook Elementary School, Newtown, Connecticut. Twenty-six people murdered, including twenty children aged six to seven years old.

June 17, 2015. Charleston, South Carolina, church. Nine people murdered.

June 12, 2016. Orlando, Florida, Pulse nightclub. Forty-nine people murdered.

October 1, 2017. Las Vegas, Nevada, concert. Fifty-eight people murdered.

February 14, 2018. Marjory Stoneman Douglas High School, Parkland, Florida. Seventeen people murdered.

November 7, 2018. Borderline Bar and Grill, Thousand Oaks, California. Twelve people murdered.

All of these places share a commonality. They are synonymous with mass murder through gun violence— and are just a small part of a list from the last twenty years that is over fifty locations long.[4] They are not the first and, sadly, have not been the last. But they are a stark reminder that the United States as a country has a terrible problem with gun violence, and not just on a mass scale. On any given day, in any given city, shootings occur. Some we hear of, and others we don't. Some are murder, some are suicide, some are a combination of both. And then there are those which are accidental. But all of them are tragic, leaving behind gaping holes in families, friendships, and communities.

Nobody knows this more than the doctors and trauma surgeons who spring into action, valiantly trying to save as many victims as possible.

Surgeons like Dr. Stephanie Bonne.

Stephanie is an assistant professor of surgery at Rutgers New Jersey Medical School in Newark. Shortly after she moved from St. Louis to New Jersey, she began working on establishing a Hospital Violence Intervention

Program and now serves as its director. Stephanie became interested in firearm injury and gun violence prevention mostly through work she was doing with the American Medical Women's Association and the American College of Surgeons. In 2018, New Jersey funded the second state gun violence research center, where she also serves as director of injury surveillance. She feels strongly that our healthcare system should play an important role in the implementation of a public health approach to gun violence prevention.

Stephanie has been an outspoken advocate on social media throughout much of her career. However, on November 7, 2018, her advocacy went viral. While stepping off an elevator during a typically busy afternoon, her phone started buzzing.

Not once. Not twice. But a steady stream of notifications from Twitter, as she was tagged on tweet after tweet by doctors and other medical professionals replying to a tweet from the National Rifle Association (NRA):

> *Someone should tell self-important anti-gun doctors to stay in their lane. Half of the articles in Annals of Internal Medicine are pushing for gun control. Most upsetting, however, the medical community seems to have consulted NO ONE but themselves.*

That tweet stopped Stephanie in her tracks. Her first thought was, "Really? Did they really say that?"

Could the NRA really believe that doctors have no role in the conversation about gun violence?

Doctors who see the victims of gun violence all the time. Doctors who plunge their hands into people's chests and abdomens—who use their hands to pump people's hearts when they stop beating on their own.

Doctors who look into people's eyes as they are dying—the very same doctors who then have to break the news to family members that their loved one isn't coming home that day...or ever again.

For Stephanie, the NRA's tweet felt like a personal attack on the integrity of her profession and every doctor who has ever tried to save a gunshot victim. As she explains, "There are only two people who can tell you the difference between what a handgun, a shotgun, and an AR-15 does to a liver, or a kidney, or a lung: me and the coroner. To the extent that those experiences are valuable, or add to the conversation, the voices of doctors are needed."

One of the things surgeons like Stephanie can tell us about gunshot trauma is the algorithms committed to memory for managing each type of injury. If a person has been "down" for longer than ten minutes with no heart rhythm, sadly, there is no point in trying to resuscitate him. If a person's heart has stopped within moments of making it to the operating room and electricity is still running through it, a surgeon can try to open the chest. But time is not the doctors' friend, as they will have about five minutes to open the chest, release the heart, fix the hole, and restart it. It's usually a heroic attempt...but honestly, very few people survive.

> *Someone should tell self-important anti-gun doctors to stay in their lane.*

When a gunshot wound is to the chest, belly, or back, a person usually must be rushed to surgery. Within fifteen minutes of arriving at the hospital, a patient should be upstairs in the operating room, anesthetized, prepped, and open, if the doctor is to have a fighting chance of saving his life. Doctors will operate very quickly because they have to. In some cases, they don't always finish the operation. If they have stabilized the bleeding, they can leave a patient's belly or chest open, cover it with a sealed plastic dressing, and take him back the next day for more surgery. In some instances, patients need surgery after surgery until the damage is repaired, but the danger, of course, is that infection can set in. And rehabilitation can take weeks or months.

Brain injuries are especially hard. The body is fine, or even perfect, but the brain is gone. There are no long goodbyes or words or kisses on the cheek. Just eyes that look straight forward and don't respond. Doctors remove the tube, the patient dies, usually in a room full of tearful family and friends.

Stephanie says, "So often, a mother or father or sibling will look at me when it's all over and say, 'Now what? What do I do now?'"

Spinal cord injuries are equally bad. As Stephanie explains, "We know, usually a few minutes after they come to the hospital, that they are paralyzed, and that it's permanent. I look sadly at their body—it will never be like this again."

The body will wear away, become riddled with bedsores and infections, and eventually succumb to an infection... but the person will be awake and know what's happening, will only watch as his body shrinks away. He walked that morning when he got out of bed, maybe even just a few minutes ago. He won't walk again, and Stephanie knows that, but he doesn't know it yet.

Sometimes the injuries are not so bad: a broken bone or a graze to soft tissue. But the fear, post-traumatic stress, and nightmares will never go away.

Stephanie sees it, but her patients don't know it yet.

Some of Stephanie's patients become her patients for a very long time. They need years of reconstructive surgeries, which she plans and provides. At every step along the way, her team is fighting for the things their patients need: rehabilitation, medical equipment, supplies, work releases, and disability. They sometimes even have to fight for proper nutrition or medications. They testify at the trials of the people who fired the guns. They really get to know their patients and see the physical and mental anguish they suffer—and the permanency of those conditions.

> *Someone should tell self-important anti-gun doctors to stay in their lane.*

As Stephanie stood by the elevator that November afternoon—mere hours before the mass shooting at Borderline Bar and Grill in Thousand Oaks, California— she scrolled through her feed while more and more friends and colleagues started posting their pictures and responses to the NRA. There were blood-soaked scrubs and shoes, bloody operating room floors, and tubes filled with fluids. Pictures and sights the general public don't typically see—these shocking, intimate moments when last breaths are drawn, and families torn apart. But for any trauma surgeon, it is the daily ebb and flow of life in the operating room, so for Stephanie, none of it was shocking.

Besides, she has a library of them on her phone, photos of livers sewn back together or intestines rerouted in creative ways: the great "saves." There is something so surreal about a trauma surgeon's phone—one minute they're scrolling through photos of their kids in their soccer uniform or ballet costume, and then the next image is of a destroyed liver.

Stephanie had seen plenty of nonsense on social media before, but this tweet from the NRA was something different—it hurt, it wounded, and it was insulting. They had in a single moment crossed a sacred line by saying "stay in your lane." In many ways, Stephanie felt, they were insinuating that doctors should simply patch up victims and send them home. Doctors shouldn't worry about *why* gunshot victims were coming in. Instead, doctors should mind their own business. Their opinions and voices did not matter.

Stephanie wasn't going to stand for that. As she notes, doctors have been on the front lines of pretty much every public health problem throughout history, all the way back to cholera-tainted wells. Doctors don't just cure people; they look for the *why* in order to use prevention. It's in their Hippocratic Oath, the most sacred words in medicine, where they say aloud that prevention is better than cure.

As her colleagues and friends continued to tweet, she too joined the chorus. It was time to swing open the doors to the operating room and really show and tell not just what gun violence looks like, but more importantly, what it leaves behind. She responded to the NRA tweet.

> *@NRA says docs should "stay in [our] lane."*
> *My lane is a son shot walking down the street*
> *with his mother. I opened his chest and re-*
> *paired his heart after it stopped, but I couldn't*
> *prevent the brain damage from lack of oxygen*
> *during CPR.*
> *#ThisisMyLane. What's yours?*

Her tweet was hard-hitting, as were the hundreds of images and tweets from other doctors—the gloves were off. The stories they held and the scenes they witnessed had to come forth; the public had a right to know what Stephanie and so many doctors dealt with on a daily basis. Before anyone can have a conversation about firearms in America, they need to start where the story ends—with the pain, suffering, and heartache.

> *@NRA says docs should "stay in [our] lane."*
> *My lane is a child who shot himself in the head*
> *when he found his father's loaded gun. I used*
> *gauze to try to cover up the brain matter*
> *coming out of his forehead when I brought his*
> *mother in to see him.*
> *#ThisisMyLane. What's yours?*

For Stephanie, there were hundreds of stories like these, memories that never leave you. And now the public was going to carry them as well.

> @NRA says docs should "stay in [our] lane."
> My lane is a pregnant woman shot in a
> moment of rage by her partner. She survived
> because the baby stopped the bullet. Have
> you ever had to deliver a shattered baby?
> #ThisisMyLane. What's yours? #Docs4Gun-
> Sense

The tweets quickly took on a life of their own, propelled across the spectrum of social media. A storm had started, and #ThisIsMyLane and #ThisIsOurLane had taken off. But the tweets and news, Stephanie feared, would rise, peak, and then like so many others, become yesterday's news—a story long forgotten, a moment over.

But Stephanie can never move on.

This is the lane she drives daily, as her hands are once again inside another abdomen or chest, trying to save a life. She can't forget about it, nor can the families that lose their loved ones.

While leaving the hospital after twenty-four hours on call, Stephanie snapped a picture of a room with a chair and posted it to Twitter. It summarized how she feels about gun violence prevention and the need to have an inclusive voice with the implementation of a public health approach. The room, sometimes known as the quiet room within the medical profession, doesn't stay quiet for long.

It is a room she hates, a room that is as bleak as the message she has to tell the parents and family members who enter.

The color of the walls is dull and institutional. A single uncomfortable chair sits to one side, across from two uncomfortable chairs that host a table next to them. There is no art on the walls, only a box of tissues, which is frequently replaced, on the table. It is a cold and stark room.

Stephanie routinely sits in many chairs: there is the one in her office, the one at her dinner table, the chair where she rocks her kids to sleep. And then there is the chair where she sits in the quiet room—the chair where she tells the parents and family members that their child or loved one did not make it and has died.

It is a chair that every doctor hates to sit in, a room every doctor hates to be in. A room where you will not find the NRA, only grieving parents and family members. A room where time stands still for so many, with every word being etched into their memory.

It is these moments that Stephanie hates, knowing that within seconds of entering that room she is about to change lives forever; that there will be inconsolable grief that will go on long after the day, the week, the years. Her words are measured, collected, and careful because she knows that every hope will hang on them, but, once delivered, every profound loss will own them.

This is her world, this is her job, this is her lane.

And it never gets easier.

As I write this story, I think about the latest mass shooting that occurred just today, where five people were murdered at the Molson Coors Beverage Company. I think about the friends and families whose lives have been shattered forever. I think about how difficult it must be for Stephanie and the hundreds of doctors who, on any given day, try to save these victims. Doctors who came into the profession to help and heal others, and yet, after giving speeches, writing papers, and working with the community, find that gun violence still exists, still grows, and ultimately still kills.

I think about Stephanie as a mother going home to hold her children, when only moments earlier she was holding another mother's child...fighting to save his life. As Stephanie notes, "I've learned to really compartmentalize work and home in my mind so I can be functional in both spaces."

But I wonder, "Could I?"

Could I be functional after the day's adrenaline rush from trying to save lives had left me? In that quiet moment when I am visited by the suffering I've seen? As Stephanie says, "I try as much as I can not to take it home, but of course it sits with you."

"We Are Not Anti-Gun.
We Are Anti-Bullet Hole."

> "We must remember that one determined
> person can make a significant difference,
> and that a small group of determined
> people can change the course of history."
>
> **—SONIA JOHNSON**

In the days immediately following the NRA's tweet,
Stephanie was invited to join a group of doctors who
were drafting a reply by her colleague Dr. Megan
Ranney, Chief Research Officer of AFFIRM, which is
the nation's leading nonpartisan network of healthcare
professionals, public health experts, and researchers who
are committed to reducing gun violence.

That open letter, which I share in part here, was
signed by more than 41,000 healthcare providers.
This letter, coupled with the viral #ThisIsMyLane
and #ThisIsOurLane campaign, has become part of a
movement of doctors like Stephanie who are using their
voices to speak out for change. Stephanie personally has
been interviewed by NowThis and has appeared on *The
Dr. Oz Show* and *CBS Sunday Morning*. Doctors across
the country continue to tweet with the #ThisIsOurLane
hashtag, while the Twitter account @ThisIsOurLane has
more than 32,000 followers to date. AFFIRM continues

its research, writing, and talks, all in the name of its mission: "The collective will of medicine will solve the gun violence epidemic."[5]

The letter is an open hand to the NRA, asking them to join healthcare professionals in finding a solution. At the time of this writing, Stephanie and her colleagues are still awaiting a response. But they will carry on speaking out until a solution to the gun violence epidemic is realized.

Excerpt from the Open Letter to the NRA from America's Health Care Providers

BE PART OF THE SOLUTION.

NRA, you dismissed the ACP's position statement on preventing death and injury from gun violence by stating, "Most upsetting, however, the medical community seems to have consulted NO ONE but themselves." We extend our invitation for you to collaborate with us to find workable, effective strategies to diminish the death toll from suicide, homicide, domestic violence, and unintentional shootings for the thousands of Americans who will one day find themselves on the wrong side of a barrel of a gun.

As Americans continue to die from gunshot wounds almost daily in our schools, our celebrations, our theaters, and in a host of other public and private settings, we invite you to help us reduce gun violence. We are not anti-gun. We are anti-bullet hole. Almost half of doctors own guns. Let's work together. You have stated that you invested in gun safety. We welcome your input.

We would like your help. However, be aware that we will move forward, with or without you. We won't be stopped. We will continue to speak on behalf of our patients and our communities. The health of all Americans is our job. Join us in our lane in protecting the health and safety of our communities, or move over!

THIS IS OUR LANE.[6]

Sometimes we get caught up in statistics, numbers, and percentages...but then we can overlook the human element. Sometimes it is the simple things that we yearn for at the end of the day, to lie beside the ones we love, to hold them long into the night, to hear them breathing beside us.

These moments are some of our most treasured, our own little gifts that we are given.

I want to finish this story with a tweet from Stephanie.

> @NRA says docs should "stay in [our] lane."
> My lane is a husband and father dying after
> weeks in the ICU. His wife asked if she could
> lay in bed next to his body one last time while
> it was still warm.
> #ThisisMyLane. What's yours?

When I read this tweet, I was profoundly saddened.
These gifts, these moments, had been taken from a wife,
who, for one last time, wanted to feel normal before she
told her children that their daddy wasn't coming home.

I just feel, and I just hope, that we as a society can come
together and do better for our families, for our children,
and for our loved ones. And it is my highest hope that
the NRA will join Stephanie and her colleagues on this
journey, so that this tweet can live in the past where
it belongs.

Stephanie's hope for the future regarding gun violence:

I think there is a lot of hope right now for what can be done.

I envision a future in which gun ownership is as safe as possible, with people understanding the risks of child access, suicide, and unintentional injury that come with it.

And I really think we need to make an investment in the root causes of violence in general—whether it's intentional interpersonal violence, domestic violence, or suicide. If we make gun ownership safe, and we decrease violence, we can decrease gun violence significantly.

I think this is possible.

Having spoken at length with people on both "sides" of the gun issue, I find there is far more that folks agree on than disagree on, so there are plenty of ways we can make a difference.

"EVERY MOMENT IS AN
OPPORTUNITY, EVERY
PERSON A POTENTIAL
ACTIVIST, EVERY MINUTE
A CHANCE TO CHANGE
THE WORLD."

—Dolores Huerta

Chapter Two

The Power
of Activism

Sometimes in life we are faced with very difficult decisions. They often present themselves quite suddenly and we react. But it is *how* we react that defines the moment.

It is how we react that defines the outcome.

When my brother was born, my mother was faced with one of these decisions. He needed immediate surgery to save his life. However, the doctors advised my parents against the procedure, saying, "He'll ruin your lives. He'll ruin your daughters' lives. You can still have more children. You should let him die."

It is in these moments, when our world seems to be crashing down around us, that we find our greatest strength. This child that my mom had carried for nine months needed to be carried more than ever. And in that moment, she decided she was going to fight for him, as she has every day since.

Though she had always been shy, my mom raised her voice and said to them, "This is my child. He's living and he's breathing right now. And I'm going to do whatever I can to give him the best life possible."

A promise that still holds true today.

Having my brother did change my parents' lives, as well as my sister's and my own. But our lives were not ruined. They have been enriched in so many ways.

That day my mom became an advocate for someone who couldn't champion himself. And through the years, she has fought for ramps in our neighborhood and at the local stores. She petitioned the city for a beach-accessible wheelchair so my brother could accompany our family on outings. And she helped other parents of disabled children with the knowledge of what to expect, what to buy, and how to become activists themselves.

My mom's actions didn't just benefit my brother. They benefited so many children and families within our community. Even to this day, they are instilled in my sister and me. It is almost as if a baton has been passed on to us to carry her work forward and champion the rights of those who can't fight for themselves.

This is the beauty of activism. It doesn't just benefit the one.

It benefits the all.

Benefiting the Planet

> "You are never too small to make
> a difference."
>
> —GRETA THUNBERG

I don't think people are born activists. I think people see
or hear something that they cannot just idly stand by
and do nothing about. Such was the case for Melati and
Isabel Wijsen, two sisters from Bali, Indonesia. When
they were just twelve and ten years old, they heard a
lesson in school about inspiring people like Nelson
Mandela, Lady Diana, and Mahatma Gandhi, and they
asked themselves, "What can we do as children living in
Bali, *now*, to make a difference?"[7]

It didn't take long for them to find the answer.

While swimming in the ocean near their home, they
would often see discarded plastic bags floating in the
water or strewn along the coast—so much so that it was
nearly impossible to swim without being entangled
in them. After doing some research on the dangers of
plastic and how other countries were dealing with it, they
discovered that more than "forty countries had already
banned or taxed plastic bags."[8]

According to the nonprofit Plastic Oceans International,
more than *eight million tons* of plastic are dumped into

the oceans each year—which obviously is eight million tons too many. And the effects have been devastating to marine life. Plastic bits have been found in the stomachs of over 90 percent of seabirds, while mammals frequently become ensnared in litter.[9]

The sisters had found their "now" and their voice, starting their organization Bye Bye Plastic Bags in 2013.

When people band together for the greater good, it's not surprising that they attract those who are like-minded. Melati and Isabel started an online petition with their friends to ban plastic bags on Bali. When they collected six thousand signatures in less than a day, they knew they were onto something.[10]

Their goal was an ambitious one million signatures, thinking that would mean they couldn't be ignored. However, they quickly realized that was "like, a thousand times a thousand," as they shared in their subsequent TED talk.[11] So they decided to think outside the box and headed to the airport because it handles millions of arrivals and departures a year. It would take several days of door-knocking and being persistent kids to get permission from the airport's manager to collect signatures beyond the customs and immigration barrier. In their first half-hour, they added another thousand signatures to their petition.[12]

School and community workshops soon followed, as did beach cleanup campaigns. But it was their idea for a hunger strike, inspired by the peaceful protest methods of Mahatma Gandhi, that really propelled their momentum forward. After their parents agreed to a compromise of fasting from sunrise to sunset, they used social media to bring awareness to their cause.[13]

It didn't take long before Bali's Governor Pastika took notice. He now had two children doing a very public hunger strike during his term. Within days, Melati and Isabel ended up standing before him, where he signed a promise to help Bali eliminate plastic, later pledging to rid the island of plastic bags by 2018. While that didn't happen, Bali's subsequent governor did sign into law a ban on all single-use plastics in 2019.[14]

Inspiration comes in many forms, but it is the call to action that has the greatest impact. Melati and Isabel saw a need and decided they, too, could make a difference. Their actions have not only benefited Bali, they have benefited the world.

And *that* is the beauty of activism. It doesn't just benefit the one, it benefits the all.

Melati's and Isabel's work continues today. Bye Bye Plastic Bags has become an international movement with teams in over twenty-five locations worldwide.[15] Both sisters have appeared at the United Nations, while Melati has spoken at the International Monetary Fund World Bank Forum, Davos 2020, and on stages across the world. As they were inspired by Nelson Mandela, Lady Diana, and Mahatma Gandhi, so too will other children be inspired by them.

As Melati and Isabel remind us, "To all the kids of this beautiful but challenging world: go for it! Make that difference. We're not telling you it's going to be easy. We're telling you it's going to be worth it. Us kids may only be 25 percent of the world's population, but we are 100 percent of the future."[16]

Benefiting Freedom

"So I have no clue, really, how I became an
activist. And I don't know how I became one
now. But all I know, and all I'm sure of, in
the future when someone asks me my story,
I will say, 'I'm proud to be amongst those
women who lifted the ban, fought the ban,
and celebrated everyone's freedom.'"

—MANAL AL-SHARIF

There are many freedoms that most women have in the
West. There's the freedom of speech, the freedom to
marry for love, and, among other things, the freedom to
drive. In the US, that latter freedom comes in our teens,
and in many ways it's a rite of passage when we get that
all-important driver's license, giving us the first taste of
independence and the ability to go anywhere.

For women in Saudi Arabia, however, these freedoms
have not always existed—and, in many cases, still don't.

Saudi women did not gain the right to drive until 2018
and it was a battle that was hard-fought. Through the
years, dozens of women had driven in protest against
the ban. But for Manal al-Sharif, 2011 was the year that
sparked her decision to act.

At that time, she was a computer scientist and a divorced single mom. One night, after visiting a doctor, she was looking for a taxi but instead found herself alone and taunted by men driving by, including one who followed her for fifteen minutes and didn't leave until she threw a rock at his car. Even though she had a car and an international driver's license, custom prohibited her from using them without a male escort. The next day she complained to a colleague about the harassment she often faced during her daily commute.[17]

She was stunned to learn from him that, while women in Saudi Arabia couldn't get driver's licenses, no actual law existed that stopped women from driving. What did exist were ultraconservative customs and beliefs that saw women as inferior and in need of a guardian. As Manal has shared, in Saudi Arabia, "They say to us: 'A woman leaves her house twice—once to her husband's house, and the second to her grave.'"[18]

A few days later, sparked by her frustration and growing anger, Manal drove her car in protest while a friend filmed her. Manal then posted her video to YouTube, calling it "Saudi Girl Driving." Within twenty-four hours, the video had garnered 800,000 views. Along with other activists, she launched the Women2Drive campaign, calling for women who had international driver's licenses to also break the ban and drive a month later, on June 17, 2011.[19]

In the following days, Manal went out driving again with her brother, to test how the authorities would respond on the big day.

It did not go well.

Manal and her brother were arrested and released after six hours at the police station, only after Manal signed a pledge not to drive again. Yet at two o'clock the next morning, Manal was taken from her home and thrown into jail for nine days. Upon her release, it was apparent that she "was the most attacked woman in Saudi Arabia." People called her office, shouting that she had "opened the doors of hell." She was threatened with rape and murder, and her picture made the front page.[20] Perhaps even worse, her son was beaten up at school because of her actions.[21]

All because she had the courage to get in a car and drive—something women did every day, in every other country on the planet.

As Manal later said, "We Saudi women need to be courageous and speak up—first with these small things, and then take action with the bigger things: it's the ripple effect."[22]

The June 17 protest went ahead and was a success, with nearly one hundred brave women driving and breaking the ban without incident.[23]

However, for Manal, the worst was yet to come.

The following year, Manal had to resign from her job, which meant she lost her house because it was subsidized by the company. She was forced to move out of the country for a new position because she had been blacklisted in Saudi Arabia, which meant leaving her son, as her ex-husband would not grant permission for Manal to take him.[24] Not only that, her brother and his family were forced to flee the country as well.[25]

In the ensuing years, Manal's fellow activists drove in protest of the ban and were also arrested. Some, including Loujain al-Hathloul, still remain in jail at the time of this writing, nearly *two years* after Saudi Arabia lifted the ban on women driving.[26]

Manal can walk and drive freely outside of Saudi Arabia, but too many of her compatriots there cannot.

Those still in prison are facing torture, electric shocks, flogging, and sexual harassment. Several may even face execution. To bring awareness to their plight and the "dismal state of women's rights" in Saudi Arabia, Manal decided to drive across America in the spring of 2019, stopping in ten cities along the way to share her story with the media and each community she visited. Her last stop coincided with her birthday in April and a protest outside the Saudi embassy in Washington, DC.[27]

Manal, who has remarried and now lives in Australia with her second husband and their son, is in self-imposed exile, as she fears arrest if she were to return to Saudi Arabia. This means she can no longer see her eldest son, and sadly her two children have never met. Her greatest hope is that one day her eldest son will know the truth of what happened and why she couldn't return to see him. This is why every award she's received, every mention in the press, has been preserved and safely tucked away in a memento box, along with a copy of her memoir, *Daring to Drive*, which Oprah named a top book to read for the summer of 2017.[28]

As history has shown us, freedom does not come easily.

Freedom is never given but has to be fought for, and there will always be great sacrifice, as Manal's story tells us. Yet she persists in her fight for the freedoms that women in Saudi Arabia—and everywhere—deserve by speaking out against the many injustices that women in her home country face daily.

The power of activism is to bring awareness, to point out the things that we cannot idly stand by and simply watch. People do not set out to be activists, but ultimately that is what they become.

So that those who follow can have a better life, a better chance, a better day.

> "Equal rights, fair play, justice, are all like the air: We all have it, or none of us has it. That is the truth of it."
>
> **—MAYA ANGELOU**

"WHAT MAKES US RESILIENT
AS HUMAN BEINGS IS THE
SHELTER OF EACH OTHER."

—Joan Borysenko

Chapter Three

Patty Turrell: Women's Journey Foundation

We all have our own stories.

Some are so painful that it is almost as if the heart cannot hold them, almost as if it will crack and break.

My story is watching my mother struggle with the lasting effects of chemotherapy, with neuropathy that has left her unsteady on her feet and a fog that causes her memory to fail her. A memory that has her family in it today but has left us worried about what the future may hold.

There are others that are filled with joy, like the way that, each morning, I awake beside the one who loves me unconditionally. Or that after forty-three years I still get to see my brother's smile; when he was born the doctors said he would have mere weeks. It is these passing days, these life stories, that pour over us and through us that are so important, where memories are made and experiences cherished. Together they are the essence of what it means to be human.

We all have our stories.

Of triumphs, of tragedies, of loss, of despair, and of love. Our stories in many ways are our experiences, but they don't always have to be the ones that define us. When women come together, we get real, we get honest, we get truthful, and we share. This is the family we choose for ourselves.

In 2002, Patty Turrell held a dinner party for some close friends. Some brought food, some brought wine, and all brought their stories. As the night unfolded, they listened to the truths, regrets, and lessons learned. It was so therapeutic to feel that they weren't alone in their experiences. Patty recalls thinking, "We should do this again, but invite more women so that they too can benefit from sharing their stories."

That night, the Women's Journey Foundation was born.

Patty wanted this foundation to host events that would be a safe place where women could come together and share their own experiences—their own stories. Their core principles include:

> To strengthen confidence and self-reliance in women and girls of all ages.
>
> To provide opportunities for women and girls and enrich their lives through multi-generational events and peer connection.
>
> To hold events designed for participants to connect

and share their experiences.

To create a path to authenticity and personal growth for women of every age.

To honor and empower women on their personal journey.

To encourage women to share those experiences for the betterment and growth of all.

Patty chose the name Women's Journey Foundation to honor our personal journeys of where we have been, where we are, and where we're going. In the first year of hosting the Women's Journey Conference, thirty-five women attended; the following year, that number doubled to seventy, and attendance multiplied from there. Mothers frequently shared story after story about the pressures that they and their daughters were facing—be it body image, self-esteem, fitting in, or finding friends. And this was even before social media was a thing.

In its early years, the Women's Journey Foundation catered to women, but as more and more mothers shared these fears, Patty realized that she needed to expand and open the doors to the younger generation. As she says, "The ultimate goal is to help young girls with how they feel about themselves and how they see themselves, because they're the future."

Sometimes we tell ourselves stories...and sometimes they are neither kind nor pleasant.

That we are not good enough, that we are not likable, not thin enough, not pretty enough...not worthy, not talented. We listen to this inner voice that can destroy us from within. As Patty notes, one of the greatest gifts we can ever give children is encouragement. It sets them on a course to succeed. And it instills in them confidence and courage, so they're not frightened to ask for help when they need it or to take risks to achieve something new or that they thought was unachievable.

Words do matter.

This is something Patty understands all too well from the moms she has met and the stories they have shared. Low self-esteem, especially in girls and teenagers, can lead to anxiety, depression, self-harm, and even suicide. In fact, in June of 2019, a study by the Journal of the American Medical Association revealed an alarming trend in the United States: suicide rates had roughly doubled for girls and young women between 2000 and 2017.[29] What's more, suicide is the leading cause of death among women ages fifteen to nineteen *worldwide*.[30]

This is why it was so important for Patty to start the annual "I Can" Girls Conference to help girls improve their self-esteem. Per the Dove Self-Esteem Project, eight out of ten girls opt out of important activities because of concerns about how they look. What's more, seven out of ten even put their health at risk by not going to the doctor or not eating when they don't like the way they look.[31]

These statistics have shaped the activities Patty includes at the conference, which is free for girls ages eight to eighteen and run entirely by volunteers. Patty and her team developed programs, workshops, and materials that address the challenges young girls face today, such as body image, social media, family dynamics, school, relationships, and most importantly, self-esteem.

One exercise they use is the "balloon" exercise, where Patty first asks the girls to write down five things they like about themselves or aspire to be. So often, as Patty shares, many of the girls find it hard to list even one positive thing about themselves—which is itself heartbreaking. After Patty and her team help the girls identify five positive traits or skills, she has them fold their slips of paper and insert them into balloons. The balloons are inflated, and the girls are then asked to write five things they *don't* like about themselves on the balloon's surface, which, unfortunately, they often have no problem doing.

After the girls break into small groups and share what they wrote, they pop their balloons, demonstrating that the bad things are smaller and less significant than what remains—the five positives about themselves.

Another great aspect of the conference is the puppy pen. If Patty notices girls who are sitting in the corner or not participating in the workshops, she will approach them and ask them to help her with a special project. "The puppies really need your help," she tells them. "Can you keep them company and give them some cuddles?"

As Patty says, "It is amazing to see the transformation in just a few minutes. The girls go into the puppy pen and their walls come down."

One year, she asked two such girls to help with the puppies. When she went back to check on the girls a bit later, they were no longer with the puppies, but instead were front and center, giggling and dancing with the Bollywood dancers. It is stunning what a little encouragement can do, and so rewarding for Patty to see this positive change take place.

On another occasion, a young girl came to the conference with a court advocate. She'd had a rough upbringing and, sadly, her mother was in a recovery home. At the end of the conference, the girl approached Patty and shared how depressed she'd been lately—even that morning, she had contemplated taking her own life. But being at the conference had given her hope, and she planned to come back the following year. The power of this conference is never fully understood until Patty hears words like these and realizes just how impactful it is for so many girls.

As she notes, "Who knows how many girls have changed their minds about suicide or harming themselves?"

One of the "I Can" Girls Conference's official role models is Darby Walker from TV's *Girl Meets World*, who was also a top-twelve finalist on season eleven of *The Voice*. Darby and her sisters attended the conference not long after moving to California from Georgia, not knowing anyone, with just some boxes, themselves, and their dreams. Darby credits the conference with giving her hope and showing her that she can do anything. She has since returned to the conference to speak to the girls about believing in their dreams.

As she says, "The advice I'd give to a girl who doesn't feel like she fits in is, 'Good for you. Embrace that.' I was never the person to fit in. Ever. And the moment I accepted myself for who I was and said, 'You know what. This is me. Take it or leave it. I'm going to be the biggest, best version of me I can be,' was the moment I was finally happy with myself."[32]

Recently, Patty and her team have created a mobile self-esteem program to take their workshops to girls in low-income areas, which they plan to expand nationally. They also work with thirty-two nonprofits and foster care agencies. And in 2018, they created a mobile self-esteem program for at-risk women that they've taken to shelters and recovery homes.

The Women's Journey Foundation conferences have benefited thousands of women and young girls through the years, especially girls from broken homes and women struggling in their lives—changing their stories for the better. The conferences have attracted bestselling authors and speakers, including Marianne Williamson, Jean Houston, Carnie Wilson, Nia Vardalos, Meredith Baxter, Marilu Henner, and the bionic woman herself, Lindsay Wagner.

And to think it all started with a small dinner party in 2002 and the power of women coming together. Which speaks to the beauty of how things sometimes work. There is no plan or goal, but sometimes magic just happens. And Patty sees this magic within each little smile and giggle. There is such a bright light that needs to be encouraged to shine, because one day these young girls will be the women who lead around the world.

As Patty says to each and every conference attendee, "Rise to your greatness, that is what you're here for."

Celebrating "HERstory"

"If we want our girls to benefit from the courage and wisdom of the women who came before them, we have to share their stories."

—SHIREEN DODSON

Some stories can be lost to time.

It is amazing to me that, of the last 3,500 years of recorded world history, less than 1 percent is devoted to women.[33]

"One can no longer deny the tremendous contribution and advancement of women," Patty explains. "We draw strength and inspiration from those who came before us. Their legacy is our story, and a truly balanced and inclusive history recognizes how important women have always been."

What's more, Patty has found a direct correlation between girls' low self-esteem and a lack of knowledge of the accomplishments of women throughout history. Bringing these stories to light, and sharing what women have achieved against remarkable odds, helps girls realize their own potential despite their own odds.

That's why another signature program of the Women's Journey Foundation is the annual Making HERstory conference, which brings to life the real accomplishments and contributions of women, historically and today. Here are just some of the amazing women Patty and her team have honored for their contributions to society—women I wish I had known more about before now.

Born in 1817, Mary Ann Bickerdyke was an organizer and chief of nursing, hospital, and welfare services for the Union Army during the American Civil War. During her tenure, she became so invaluable that General Ulysses S. Grant actually gave her a pass so that she could travel anywhere in his command. She is credited with overseeing the set-up of three hundred field hospitals with an emphasis on sanitation and was later known as "Mother" Bickerdyke for her compassion toward the wounded and sick. Of note, she is also credited with having several incompetent officers and physicians dismissed, which, for the time, speaks to how well-respected she was. Mary Ann was a valued asset both on and off the battlefield, assisting veterans long after the war with pension claims.[34]

Mary Ann Bickerdyke's story is not as well-known as General Grant's, but both played a great role in the Civil War. I wonder if more women through the years would have been inspired to follow in her footsteps and contribute to the medical profession if her story was shared as frequently as his.

Similarly, I wish I had heard more about NASA's Katherine Johnson before the movie *Hidden Figures* was released a few years ago. Katherine, a talented African American mathematician, performed trajectory analysis for Alan Shepard's 1961 mission *Freedom 7*, which was the first human space flight for the United States. She also coauthored a report in 1960 with engineer Ted Skopinski that featured equations for an orbital space flight in which the landing position was also stated— the first time a woman in the Flight Research Division received credit for writing this type of report.[35]

Computers were introduced to NASA during that time, and they were relied upon for calculations that would control the trajectory of the capsule in John Glenn's *Friendship 7* mission from liftoff to splashdown. The astronauts, however, were very wary, because these computers were prone to hiccups and blackouts.

As they started their pre-flight checklist, John Glenn famously asked engineers to "get the girl."[36]

Katherine was summoned, given the same data as the computers, and asked to run the equations by hand on her desktop calculating machine, with John Glenn declaring, "If she says they're good, then I'm ready to go."[37]

John Glenn's flight was a success, and it was Katherine Johnson he trusted with his life that day. She was the person who put him into orbit—and the history books. And while I vividly remember lessons about him in school throughout my childhood, never once did I hear Katherine Johnson's name mentioned or learn about her tremendous accomplishments—especially in an era when a darker history was unfolding across America, segregation.

You can never extinguish a human spirit that burns so brightly.

For her contributions to mathematics and NASA, she was presented with the Presidential Medal of Freedom, America's highest civilian honor, in 2015, at the age of 97. While I was writing this chapter, Katherine Johnson passed away at the age of 101. I reflect upon her story, including the horrors she experienced in her lifetime with segregation: having to sit at the back of the bus, using separate bathrooms and separate drinking fountains, and being one of only three students to integrate graduate schools in West Virginia.[38]

But she rose above all of that adversity—and nevertheless, she persisted, paving the way for others.

Just as sharing the stories of women in science and mathematics is important, so too is sharing the stories of the many women who have fought for freedom, equality, and the right to vote around the world. These brave women have often endured verbal and physical attacks as they fought for their rights—for equal rights.

Patty often marvels at these women, who knew they might not see these rights in their lifetimes, but forged ahead anyway so that, as she says, "Women in the future could have more."

One such woman was Alice Paul, a leading advocate in the women's suffrage movement that helped secure the Nineteenth Amendment to the US Constitution, giving women the right to vote in 1920. This accomplishment, however, was not won easily. Alice and eight thousand other women marched from the Capitol to the White House on March 3, 1913, the day before President-elect Woodrow Wilson's inauguration, only to have Wilson meet with them two weeks later and say it was not time for a Constitutional amendment.[39]

Four years later, Alice Paul and more than a thousand "Silent Sentinels" began picketing the White House, carrying signs that read, "Mr. President, how long must women wait for liberty?" These women were attacked both verbally and physically and were even arrested for obstructing traffic. Alice Paul was sentenced to jail for seven months and organized a hunger strike in protest.[40]

In 1918, President Woodrow Wilson finally announced his support for giving women the right to vote. It would take another two years for Congress and the required thirty-six states to approve the amendment, which was ratified into law in 1920—marking its centennial anniversary in 2020.[41]

Once the battle for the right to vote had been won, Alice turned her sights to equal rights for women in general. The Equal Rights Amendment was first introduced in Congress in 1923 and was reintroduced in every session of Congress from that date until 1972, when it was finally passed.[42]

"I never doubted that equal rights was the right direction. Most reforms, most problems are complicated. But to me there is nothing complicated about ordinary equality."

—ALICE PAUL, 1972

And yet, the struggle continues. It wasn't until 2020 that the required thirty-eighth state ratified the amendment, when Virginia did so in January. And as of the time of this writing, court challenges remain.[43]

As I researched Alice's story, I was moved by her strength and courage and by those who stood beside her for equality. And yet, I am horrified at what they had to endure for their rights...and what women in some parts of the world still endure in the fight for freedom and equality.

Alice's story is often lost in the classrooms of history—absent from the books of accomplishment and courage and from the studies of human strife and injustice. Her name and her actions should never be forgotten. They honor every woman today, as they did then, and should be immortalized within the eternal flame that lives in each of us.

> "Each time a girl opens a book and finds a womanless history, she learns she is worth less."
>
> **—MYRA POLLACK SADKER**

This is why it's so important to Patty that the Women's Journey Foundation is a collaborative partner with the National Women's History Museum. And thanks to the passing of the Smithsonian Women's History Museum Act by the House of Representatives on February 11, 2020—by a vote of 374 to 37—we are one step closer to seeing a museum dedicated solely to women's history beside the other great museums that line the mall in Washington, DC.

The bill's lead sponsors, Congresswoman Carolyn B. Maloney (D-NY), Congressman Brian Fitzpatrick (R-PA), Congresswoman Brenda Lawrence (D-MI), and Congresswoman Eleanor Holmes Norton (D-DC), celebrated its passage with this statement:

> For too long, women's history has been left out of the telling of our nation's history. Today, the House of Representatives took an important first step to change that. Women are part of every American moment, and their contributions should be recognized and celebrated.
>
> By creating a Smithsonian museum dedicated to telling American women's history, we can inspire future generations to make history themselves. Representation matters. Let's make sure that every child can see themselves in their heroes and role models. We will be working together to ensure swift Senate passage of this bill.[44]

The companion bill in the Senate is sponsored by Senators Susan Collins (R-ME) and Dianne Feinstein (D-CA), who noted, "American women have made invaluable contributions to our country in every field, including government, business, medicine, law, literature, sports, entertainment, the arts, and the military. Telling the history of American women matters, and a museum recognizing these achievements and experiences is long overdue."[45]

However, the stories of women have never been easy.

We have had to fight for every right we have today. Here in the US, our fight continues for things like equal pay for equal work and, increasingly, our right to choose. Many women around the world have to fight for so much more—and it is a fight that persists.

Today the Senate's version of the Smithsonian Women's History Museum Act must reach the desks of men before it becomes law—not unlike a hundred years ago, when our right to vote fell into the hands of men. It is my greatest hope that future bills pertaining to women will one day soon cross the desk of a woman.

Patty, like millions of women in recent years, has marched for women's rights. One thing I've particularly admired is that she has put our past heroes in front of us, marching dressed as a suffragette to honor the women who marched for us more than a hundred years ago. In many ways, she is dressing from the past to inspire future generations, especially younger women.

And yet, one of the saddest stories still continues...the number of girls and women taking their lives worldwide.

It is for all these reasons that it is so important to have organizations like the Women's Journey Foundation. It's so important to have a museum dedicated to women's struggles, accomplishments, stories, and history, so that we can feel a sense of strength, camaraderie, and sisterhood with those who have come before us. It's so important to see women in politics and in leadership roles worldwide to help limit the misogyny and abuse that has a direct correlation to suicide.

I'm excited to see Patty expanding the Women's Journey Foundation, so she can have greater reach among at-risk girls and women, to help them rewrite their stories.

And so to Patty, the tireless missionary enriching the lives of so many, I say, "Thank you."

Women's Journey Foundation

Since 2006, the Women's Journey Foundation
has helped thousands of girls overcome feelings
of inadequacy and self-doubt. In their own words,
they've learned:[46]

- 💬 "To believe in myself." *Hunter H.*, age ten

- 💬 "That I have the courage I never knew I had."
  Sarah W., age thirteen

- 💬 "I'm amazing in many ways." *Kasidy W.*,
  age twelve

- 💬 "Be yourself and women are as great as men."
  Nicole O., age ten

- 💬 "To be myself and women are good at things
  too." *Natalie G.*, age eleven

- 💬 "That you should follow your dreams even
  when people tell you no." *Cailyn*, age nine

- 💬 "That no matter what obstacles come in your
  path of life, if you have faith in yourself and
  enough determination, you can overcome
  anything." *Alesha A.*, age sixteen

- 💬 "People talk to us and listen." *Janice C.*,
  age seventeen

- "To not give up on myself and that it is possible for anyone to be something in life." *Ingrid L.*, age seventeen

- "To love myself no matter what. I also learned that everyone is special." *Victoria F.*, age fourteen

- "If I trust myself, I can do better at everything I do." *Sierra H.*

- "It takes confidence, desire, and determination to achieve that which seems impossible." *Rebecca F.*, age seventeen

"THE GREATNESS OF A COMMUNITY IS MOST ACCURATELY MEASURED BY THE COMPASSIONATE ACTIONS OF ITS MEMBERS."

—Coretta Scott King

Chapter Four

~~~~~~~~

The Power of Community

The beginning of 2020 brought with it excitement as we looked to a new decade...but it was an excitement that would be short-lived.

Within just a few months, the COVID-19 virus pandemic had spread around the world. With schools, restaurants, theaters, sporting events, and even some countries' borders closed, and millions of people all but quarantined in their homes—life as we'd known it had changed.

But in the midst of these unknown and worrying times, we saw the beauty and power of community.

For Italy, one of the earliest, hardest-hit nations that was put under a strict lockdown with many people isolated at home, there were pictures of mothers and daughters hanging inspirational signs on balconies and gates with the phrase *"andrà tutto bene,"* or "everything will be alright."[47] Similarly, the #FromMyWindow movement encouraged children to create signs for their windows to bring a smile to people's faces.

On balconies throughout Siena in Tuscany, voices filled the air with the popular tune, *"Il Canto della Verbena"* ("The Song of Verbena"), with neighbors up and down the streets joining in to raise people's spirits.[48] News channels promoted a "flash mob" where Italians were encouraged to turn off their lights and use a phone or flashlight at a designated time to illuminate the sky.[49]

Stories from China also showed neighbors singing patriotic songs from their windows and balconies,[50] while a social media campaign in Spain resulted in residents giving the nation's healthcare workers a national round of applause.[51]

England followed suit, with a #ClapForOurCarers tribute to the nation's healthcare workers, as people all across the country applauded from their windows and doorsteps at the designated time.[52] Hundreds of thousands of people also volunteered to help England's National Health Service by delivering food and medicines, phoning those in quarantine, and driving patients to appointments.[53]

Meanwhile, in Ohio, two young children staged a cello concert on their porch for their seventy-eight-year-old neighbor, who was self-isolating due to concerns about the virus.[54] Scores of free online art and exercise classes and museum virtual tours were offered for kids and adults alike who were at home amid school closures and lockdowns.

Around the world—amid stories of hoarding and price gouging—there were also stories of people checking on their elderly neighbors, offering to drop off medicines and groceries. Many stores even adjusted hours so that the elderly and most vulnerable could shop first each morning. Community groups sprang up on social media so people could post offers of or requests for help. And athletes and celebrities began donating money to help those whose jobs were lost due to closures.

This is the healing power of humanity.

This is the healing power of community.

And the power of community comes in many forms and across many ages.

In 2014, residents of Flint, Michigan, knew from the rust-colored water that something was wrong with their water supply. Months of denials from officials followed, until a local pediatrician, Dr. Mona Hanna-Attisha, proved that children were being poisoned as they were exposed to high levels of lead.[55]

Flint resident Mari Copeny was just eight years old when she and her siblings learned they had to stop turning on the tap and rely solely on bottled water. She decided to write President Obama a letter and ask him to come to Flint to see what was happening firsthand, even though the chances of him reading it were small. Yet, about a month and a half later, Mari's mother heard from a White House staffer. President Obama had read Mari's letter and had decided to come to Flint.[56]

Sometimes the smallest of voices can have the greatest of impacts.

Mari's letter and President Obama's subsequent visit helped bring national attention to the Flint water crisis. Since 2016, Mari—also known as Little Miss Flint—has helped raise over $500,000 for more than 25,000 children in her community of Flint and elsewhere, providing school supplies, toys, bikes, clean water, and more. And when Michigan ceased paying for bottled water for Flint residents, Mari raised an additional $280,000, distributing over a million bottles of water. Since the summer of 2019, Mari has also partnered with a water filtration company to bring water filters to communities across the US that have experienced toxic water.[57]

However, this story is ongoing for Flint, which has one of the highest poverty rates in the country, and for the many communities around the world that do not have access to clean water.

From the heyday of the crisis in Flint alone, Dr. Mona Hanna-Attisha estimates that 14,000 children "under the age of six may have been exposed to lead in their water."[58] Three years after the crisis began, sadly, the number of third graders who passed Michigan's standardized literacy test plunged from 41 percent to just 10 percent. To this day, many parents in Flint still bathe their kids in bottled water, warmed first on the stove.[59]

In January 2019, Dr. Mona Hanna-Attisha started a registry for the thousands of kids exposed to lead in

Flint's water. The registry refers kids to specialists for tests to help determine if they've suffered any developmental delays.

And the preliminary findings are startling.

As Dr. Mona Hanna-Attisha shared with *60 Minutes*, "Before the crisis, about 15 percent of the kids in Flint required special education services. But of the 174 children who went through the extensive neuro-exams, specialists determined that 80 percent will require help for a language, learning, or intellectual disorder."[60]

So far, the registry she started has already connected two thousand children to critical services like speech and occupational therapy, which some may need for their entire lives.[61]

While this story received national attention, in a world of competing news cycles, headlines can move on. And yet, it is people like Mari Copeny and Dr. Mona Hanna-Attisha who champion the community with their ongoing efforts. When a problem or need arises, it is always our heroes who rise to the challenge of finding solutions—no matter their age.

No matter the cause.

The Power of Education

"When girls are educated, they lift up their families, their communities, and their countries."

—OBAMA FOUNDATION

It is said that one of the best gifts you can ever give a child is an education.

And yet, as the Obama Foundation shares, nearly ninety-eight million adolescent girls do not attend school, which is a great loss for communities around the world.[62]

The reasons for this can vary widely, and all of them are tragic. In some areas, long-waged wars and conflicts mean commutes are just too dangerous to attempt, especially if the closest school is hours away. Poverty, of course, is a debilitating factor for many as well, if families simply lack the fees to pay.[63]

Even stigma around menstruation can keep girls away from school during their menstrual cycles—especially if the school does not have adequate bathroom facilities. So often, girls can fall behind in these circumstances and, sadly, stop attending school altogether.[64]

But sometimes, there is a hurdle that is perhaps greater than all of these. Sometimes, the grip of patriarchy that has held tight its grasp on communities for generations is the biggest obstacle that girls face. The ability to read and write can let a young mind soar, as well as provide self-confidence and a better future, but for some this gift is never given.

For some girls, the hardest thing can be telling their parents they want to go to school.

Because for generations, girls have been expected to do the household chores or even assume household duties full-time once they reach adolescence. It is the daughters, not the sons, who are asked to clean dishes or bring refreshments to guests who come over. It is the daughters, not the sons, who serve. In fact, girls fifteen and younger around the world have been found to spend *160 million hours* more than boys on household chores each day.[65]

Even worse, the practice of child marriage is still far too common. It is estimated that twelve million girls are married before their eighteenth birthday each year—meaning that twenty-three girls *every minute* become child brides.[66]

Women now make up two-thirds of the world's 750 million illiterate adults.[67] And the cycle of patriarchy, poverty, and abuse continues, just as it has for mothers and grandmothers and generations past.

And yet, there is always a better way.

Universal secondary education could not only eliminate child marriage, per World Bank reports, it would also mean that 420 million people could rise out of poverty.[68]

And it is the power of community and women banding together that are working to make this a reality.

Recently, the Obama Foundation created the Girls Opportunity Alliance to help these communities and the women who are working so hard to help girls around the world. One such leader is Dr. Urvashi Sahni, a women's and children's rights activist and founder of the Study Hall Educational Foundation (SHEF) in Lucknow, India. SHEF's mission is "to provide quality education to underprivileged girls and youth in urban and rural India," with a particular focus on educating and empowering girls.[69]

One of several programs from SHEF is the Prerna Girls School, which is a K–12 school for underprivileged girls from neighboring slums and communities. In 2003, the school was founded with eighty students and four teachers, and now it helps over eight hundred girls receive an education...and helps them break the cycle of patriarchy.[70]

As part of the curriculum, girls learn specific ways to communicate about things that impact their daily lives. For instance, ways to speak with their parents to help them understand that household chores can be shared responsibilities between sons and daughters. That the mentality of "it's always been this way" doesn't mean it has to stay this way.[71]

"All girls at Prerna have scary and inspiring stories. These girls have brutal home lives. Lives that are hard, violent, abusive, powerless, and very poor. Many of these girls are not touched at home, except to be beaten. Their fault is being female, lower-caste, and poor. Not much further you can fall in the universal power ladder. They have no control over their lives, their earnings, and their bodies. Yet they engage in their studies, come to school regularly, and put in the work they need to do. This is their hope to get a new life…to fulfill a dream that they have dared to have."[72]

—SHEF Prerna Girls School

Equally important is SHEF's Prerna Boys School, as the curriculum helps boys recognize that they can be part of the solution for the way women are treated. The boys also attend critical dialogue sessions to help change the mindset that women should always be at men's beck and call. Teachers work with the boys to help them understand that their sisters, and women in general, should be seen as equals.[73]

In her interview for the YouTube Original *Why 98 Million Adolescent Girls Aren't In School #CreatorsForChange*,

Dr. Urvashi Sahni shared that the boys are beginning to learn a different idea of manhood, where they can be the ones bringing a glass of water to their sisters or seeing girls as persons with feelings. Some students have even been able to change their friends' perspectives.[74]

Dr. Urvashi Sahni is just one of many women working to give a voice to the voiceless, especially in the poorer and rural areas where even a young girl can dare to dream of a better life.

I hope her work and the work of so many women around the world can continue in the face of the COVID-19 pandemic, so that this much-needed progress will not be lost and the story of patriarchy can finally come to an end.

In this unknowing time, there is one thing that rises above all others, and that is to be kind, to be generous, and to be charitable. And, just as women have always adapted in the midst of hardship, we will continue to band together, carry on, and support the power of community.

> "I raise up my voice—not so I can shout but so that those without a voice can be heard... we cannot succeed when half of us are held back."
>
> —MALALA YOUSAFZAI

"THERE ARE SOME THINGS WOMEN DON'T DO. THEY DON'T BECOME POPE OR PRESIDENT OR GO DOWN TO THE ANTARCTIC."

—Harry Darlington

Chapter Five

Antarctic Fire Angels: Ordinary Women Doing Extraordinary Things

There are stories that tell of courage and bravery, while others speak of endurance and unparalleled strength. But when you have a story that encompasses all these qualities, you have a story that must be read—a story that must be told.

This is the story of the Antarctic Fire Angels.

In November of 2023, six female firefighters from England and Wales will start a 1,180-mile (1,900-kilometer) trek across Antarctica. Not for fame or fortune, but all in the name of charity. To shine a light on mental health. And to bring awareness to women around the world that we are remarkable and can accomplish anything.

Team leader Nakita Ross joined the London Fire Brigade when she was just twenty years old. She first found her love of the uniformed services in her teens as an Air Cadet, and though her parents wanted her to attend Sandhurst, the royal military academy, to become an army officer, like so many of us, she left school uncertain about what she wanted to do.

Then her father, a thirty-three-year veteran of the police force, had a massive stroke. When he first came around, he could no longer speak English and had reverted to his native tongue, Dutch. He also no longer recognized five of his eight children, only the youngest three.

For Nakita, seeing her dad's daily struggle with even the simplest tasks often left her in tears and with a sorrow that words failed to convey.

Nakita knew she needed to determine what to do with her future, which would also allow her to help her mum, who was left caring for her dad and eight children. She applied for positions with the Metropolitan Police and the London Fire Brigade and was awarded both—it was a crossroads.

In a quiet moment with her dad, who was slowly recovering, she asked for his advice. He said, "If I could have done any other job than being a police officer, it would have been a firefighter."

We all have a calling in life, and Nakita had just heard hers.

One of the highlights of Nakita's thirteen-year career thus far is becoming London's first female Urban Search and Rescue (USAR) instructor. Another was meeting Georgina Gilbert, a twenty-year veteran firefighter from Wales, during a USAR workshop at the 2018 Women in the Fire Service (WFS) event.

When Georgina joined the fire service, it was one of the few uniformed careers in which women could perform all the same roles as men. It's probably not a surprise that Wonder Woman was Georgina's only role model growing up. To this day, she doesn't leave the house without a Lego Wonder Woman miniature in her pocket.

It is funny how some people just fall into each other, becoming lifelong friends in a moment. Nakita and Georgina hit it off instantly. Both are highly competitive, love adventure, and are always up for a great challenge. At the end of the event, they vowed to keep in touch.

Little did they know then, but one of the greatest challenges would present itself the following year, when Nakita and Georgina attended the 2019 WFS event. The keynote speaker, Sophie Montague, was one of six women from the British army who became the largest all-female group to ski across the Antarctic coast to coast. The "Ice Maidens" completed their thousand-mile journey in sixty-two days.[75]

Sophie spoke about how she wanted to show women what women can achieve. This was music to Georgina's ears, as a HeForShe ambassador and a firm believer in inclusion and gender equality. This was also a lightbulb moment for Nakita, who thought, "Why can't we do something like this? No female team of firefighters has done anything like this."

When Nakita and Georgina met up after the event, they looked at each other and spontaneously blurted, "Shall we do this Antarctic thing?!" Immediately, they made a beeline for Sophie to get more information.

> "We're here for a reason. I believe a bit of the reason is to throw little torches out to lead people through the darkness."
>
> **—WHOOPI GOLDBERG**

There are some moments that defy all odds and become life-changing. Almost as if there is some universal calling or inevitable fate that brings people together...people who, when combined, will change worlds.

A month later, Nakita and Georgina met to compare notes and start planning. The sheer size of the organization for the challenge was daunting. There was the cost (likely half a million pounds) and the obvious need for sponsorships. There was the logistics of getting to and from the Antarctic and planning a route never before taken by an all-female team. There was the three-year commitment to the level of training that would be required for a journey that would last seventy days with temperatures as low as -58 degrees Fahrenheit (-50 Celsius), including strength and conditioning, crevasse training, line rescue, and Nordic skiing with loaded pulks or sleds to carry supplies.

And most important of all, there was building the right team of female firefighters. A group of women who would together endure some of the harshest conditions on earth, both physically and mentally. A group of women who would entrust each other with their lives.

Over the next few months, they found four incredible women to join them on this journey, each one bringing her own excitement and love of adventure into the fray. Each one wanting to prove to herself and to women everywhere that "ordinary women can do extraordinary things."

Alison Kibblewhite was the first woman to become a full-time firefighter in Wales over twenty-five years ago, setting the stage for other women to follow. She now serves as a Temporary Assistant Chief Fire Officer in South Wales, where she manages forty-seven fire stations, fire control, community safety, and business fire safety. While most people think about a leisurely retirement as they near the ends of their careers, that couldn't be further from the truth for Alison. She sees being a part of the Antarctic Fire Angels as a wonderful opportunity to leave a legacy for future women in the fire service, as well as a way to set an example for her grandchildren.

Beci Newton, a Crew Manager at Cardiff Central Fire Station in South Wales, was instantly inspired by the challenge. It was always a childhood dream of hers to be an explorer and to stand on a part of the earth that no other human had—though, as the mum of a nine-year-old and a six-year-old, it took her a while to say yes to the invitation. For a mother, there is no greater need than knowing her children are safe and sound, and she didn't want her absence to have a negative impact on them. After many discussions with her supportive husband, Matt, ultimately, she decided that this is a once-in-a-lifetime opportunity. Besides, she also wants her kids to grow up knowing that nothing is beyond their reach.

From the London-based crew, Rebecca Rowe has always had sports in her veins. She has competed in the rugby World Cup and Six Nations for Wales, won world championships in surf lifesaving, and rowed for Great Britain. After her sporting career was cut short twice by injury, her dream of becoming an Olympian was to go unrealized. Part of the allure of joining the team is to have another opportunity to set a record for the history books. Her support team includes her mini sausage dog, George, who will be cheering her on from the comfort of her flat.

Nikki Upton has always sought out a challenge, be it a ten-kilometer swim, a seventy-five-mile bike ride, or a boxing fight in front of 1,200 people. Without knowing it, Nikki had been crying out for a project, so when she was asked to join the team, there wasn't a single part of her that considered saying no. Nikki wonders at these six women, all within the fire service, who will be marching across the landscape of ice, proving that women can conquer both extremes. She says that, if even one woman is inspired by this venture, it'll make the three months she has to go without Twiglets all worth it.

Shining a Light on Mental Health

To inspire the next generation to explore and smash stereotypical barriers that would otherwise stop them from doing anything they put their minds to and raise awareness of the impact of mental health on firefighters.

—ANTARCTIC FIRE ANGELS EXPEDITION VISION

Our firefighters and first responders are always looked to as heroes and champions, but they crack and they break and they struggle like you and me. Sometimes we forget that they, too, are human.

In this modern age, whenever there is a disaster, as the news cycle spreads, cell phones start ringing with loved ones trying in vain to get through, whether to their child at school or their spouse on the way home from work or their friend out for the night. But it's the first responders and firefighters who are often the recipients of each call, an orchestra of all-too-familiar ring tones and pop songs that just don't stop.

These constant, unrelenting calls that come from pockets, jackets, and purses while they try to triage who can be saved assault even the strongest of firefighters' mental defenses with the guilt that they're keeping a secret from the victims' loved ones...with the guilt of knowing some of the wounded will never make it home again.

For Nakita, it was the call (or shout as it's known in England) to a tram derailment on November 9, 2016, in Croydon, London, that left its mark. It was a rainy, dark morning when tram 2551 rounded a sharp corner going significantly faster than the recommended speed limit. Apparently, the driver had fallen asleep, causing the tram to derail. Seven people were killed, and at least fifty-one were injured, some seriously.

According to the reports, the tram rolled three times, ending up on its side. Several of the victims were ejected from the carriage via the windows, with some pinned underneath. Survivors tell of bodies and blood everywhere and being unable to get out. One man recalls coming to and all that was left of his seat mate was his boot. More than a hundred emergency service workers spent the better part of six hours trying to free everyone from the tram.[76]

"War zone." "Horror film." Those were just two descriptors commuters used when recalling the day.[77]

And then of course there was the Grenfell Tower fire, another shout for both Nakita and Nikki that took its toll. In the early morning hours of June 14, 2017, a fire started on the fourth floor of the twenty-three-story residential tower. Grenfell Tower was designed so that a fire would be contained in a single flat. But within thirty minutes of the first firefighters' arrival on the scene, that design proved to be deadly wrong as the fire compromised the kitchen window and quickly spread to the outside of the tower.[78]

One witness recounted seeing a mother throw her baby from a window to a person below, so that the baby could live when she knew she would not. Others recall residents standing by windows with their cell phones illuminated so that they could be seen and rescued, while others waved towels. Sadly, they were only met with a wall of flame.[79]

In less than four hours, the entire building was engulfed. While firefighters rescued sixty-five people from the tower that day, many residents became trapped and sought refuge with neighbors on higher floors when they couldn't make it down the stairs. Twenty-four people died on the top floor alone, while seventy-two people perished in total. It was one of the greatest losses of life in London in modern times.[80]

Nothing can quite prepare you for what you see on a shout—but then again, nothing can quite prepare you for how it leaves you.

I think about Nakita, Georgina, Alison, Beci, Rebecca, Nikki, and every firefighter who battles a blaze or attends an accident, and the sheer agony that must occur when they realize that they can't save everyone. The personal defeats that stay with them long after the flames are gone.

Firefighters and first responders are considered very much like superheroes—they run *into* buildings and dangers that everyone else is running *from*. They are the gentle voice when the world seems to be imploding, or the shout in the darkness that guides us into the light.

But sometimes, these helping hands are the hands that need to be helped. Sometimes we hide behind our laughs and smiles, but deep within us a storm is raging. Sometimes it is harder to take the hand that is offered than it is to admit the truth that we are drowning.

For many first responders and firefighters alike, being in extremely stressful situations can lead to mental health conditions, including post-traumatic stress disorder (PTSD). Per the Mayo Clinic, PTSD is "a mental health condition that's triggered by a terrifying event—either experiencing it or witnessing it. Symptoms may include flashbacks, nightmares, and severe anxiety, as well as uncontrollable thoughts about the event."[81]

PTSD can often lead to insomnia, depression, isolation, and even thoughts of self-harm. If left undiagnosed or untreated, the results can prove devastating, leaving the person emotionally numb, detached from family and friends, and hopeless about the future.

For Nakita, PTSD is very real, having been diagnosed after the Grenfell Tower fire. For both the Croydon tram crash and Grenfell fire, she was one of the firefighters responsible for recovering bodies. And while she had done this before in her career, it was not to this scale and not twice in an eight-month period, with both incidents extensively documented in the media. It was almost like there was no escaping these two tragedies.

In England, one of the places firefighters can turn when they need help is the Fire Fighters Charity, which the team are raising money for as part of this journey. The Fire Fighters Charity was set up and designed specifically to help firefighters with their physical and mental health and social well-being. As they say, they "rescue the rescuers," ensuring they get the right support in the right way and at the right time.[82]

The charity is near and dear to the hearts of everyone on the team and was there for Nakita when she tore ligaments in her ankle and for Nikki when she broke her foot. Through this expedition, they want to give back to a charity that is devoted to helping members of the firefighting community, and to bring attention to the tremendous work they continue to do.

Smashing Stereotypes

> "We want to leave a legacy for all those girls and young women who have ever been told, 'You can't do that.' Proving to women what women can do."
>
> **—ANTARCTIC FIRE ANGELS**

It's not every day that six women ski across the Antarctic to raise awareness about equality and inclusion, but it is every day that women are excluded from fundamental rights and opportunities. Nakita notes that, "Of the 35,000 firefighters in the United Kingdom, only 6 percent are women." Equal pay remains elusive in many fields, and at the current pace, it is estimated that the pay gap will remain for another sixty-two years in the UK.[83]

This is a worldwide problem and struggle for many women. While the fist of patriarchy has loosened its grip in many places around the world, in others it remains clasped. This grip should resemble an open hand, so that dreams and hopes for both men and women are equally held, equally shared...equally achieved.

The team wants to encourage women of all ages to consider a career in the fire service or other nontraditional fields, which they credit with giving them inner strength and confidence. They hope their expedition will have a positive impact on future recruitment, especially in their lifetime.

They also want to change people's perspectives about the fact that a woman can be in charge. As Alison notes, owners of burning buildings sometimes approach her male colleagues, and in turn they will point to her and say, "She's the boss." Even after seeing "Incident Commander" noted on her helmet, some people still want to keep speaking with a man.

Above all, the team want to encourage women to push themselves for whatever they wish to achieve. To rise, to stand and shoulder any prejudices that are presented, for within each of us there is an inner strength that can conquer any injustice.

The team has pledged to raise money for the Fawcett Society, which is the UK's leading charity fighting for gender equality and women's rights, including campaigns that aim to close the gender pay gap, secure equal power among elected officials, challenge attitudes, and defend hard-fought women's rights post-Brexit (such as rights for pregnant women, working parents, and women escaping violence).[84]

They will also be raising money for the Harlequins Foundation, which focuses on using the power of sports to drive positive change (the whole team love their sport!). Their two core programs are SWITCH, which encourages girls to get involved and excel in sport, and METTLE, which challenges stigmas around mental health issues and helps develop mental resilience in young people.[85]

The Journey Begins

"There are challenges that make us rise, that test every aspect of our being. Where we fight our very selves and come through the other side unbeaten."

—J. T. WILLIAMS

The Antarctic hosts some of the most extreme weather conditions known on earth, where temperatures can fall to a -58 degrees Fahrenheit (-50 Celsius), coupled with sixty-mile-per-hour winds and unrelenting white-out conditions. Each member of the team will be subjecting herself to a rigorous training scheme leading up to their trip. It will be this training that could be the difference between life and death.

Some of their training exercises will be grueling circuits, weightlifting, and cardio, while others will involve strength, conditioning, stamina, and endurance. Their exposure, navigation, and medic training are crucial, as is learning the skills needed to navigate the terrain. They will travel to Scotland, Norway, and Canada for crevasse training, ski training, and two-week polar expeditions.

At the time of this writing, the team is in Scotland, learning cross-country skiing at the Huntly Nordic Outdoor Centre, a new skill for many of them. When the weekend began, they could hardly stay on the tracks, but, as they say, a little bit of motivation comes in many guises, and humor really is the key. The team would always get a laugh when Nakita would shout her motto "get up or you die" as they were helped up after falling while trying to master the art of Nordic skiing. By the end of the weekend, they were well on their way with cross-country skiing, and Nakita could rest her vocal cords.

The spirit of camaraderie is so important, but so is a toast to a job well done. To celebrate their first team training trip, they bought a bottle of Shackleton Whisky, the spirit supplied to the 1907 British Antarctic Expedition. On the team's Instagram account, Shackleton Whisky wrote to encourage them with their training. It is easy to get behind people doing great things for great causes.

Nakita, Rebecca, and Nikki are also getting ready to run London's half-marathon supporting the Fawcett Society, and, if the team hits its two thousand pound fundraising goal beforehand, they've offered to run while wearing their firefighting gear. Judging by their tenacity, it won't slow them down much!

They would also love for people to train with them. They want to give everyone—women especially—a sense of the rigors of their preparations, so we can also prove to ourselves how capable we are. For me personally, I've set a goal to join them during one of their training exercises, to help mark my turning fifty the year before their trip. I'll be proud if I can keep pace the first mile before I watch them head off into the distance. Thank goodness for taxis!

"What does it take to be the first female anything? It takes grit, and it takes grace."

—MERYL STREEP

Instead of following in other people's footsteps, the team want to pave their own path. They intend to ski a coast-to-coast route never before traveled by an all-female team. They will begin their journey at Berkner Island, traversing to the South Pole. From there, they will trek to the Axel Heiberg Glacier, followed by the Titan Dome, and then on to the Ross Ice Shelf, where they will be picked up.

While writing this story, I have often paused for a moment to take in just exactly what these brave women are doing—and why they are doing it. I have tried to imagine what they will face as they ski in tandem, alone with their thoughts for ten to twelve hours each day—the utter isolation of the landscape where no animals are seen and no birds fly. Their skis slicing through snow and ice the only sound to drown out the noise of the mind. The pull of their pulks that tires the back and exhausts the legs.

Then, of course there is the freezing air that will surround them—that bites the face and chips away at morale, taunting them to quit, to give in. There will also be days that host blue skies and diamond-like snow, the days where, upon opening their tent, they see a surreal beauty. But then these days can turn on them and leave them huddled in their tent as the howling winds pass through, changing the landscape once again to an inhospitable place that tries to break them.

As their journey continues, their bodies will change. They will start to weaken as weight is lost; there will be a constant battle of losing calories while they desperately try to replace them. There will be the constant battle of the mind to soldier on and complete the journey as the body calls out to rest...to stop...because every part of it aches. As they are reminded by Nakita to "get up or die."

There is no doubt that the journey will be grueling both physically and mentally. When faced with tremendous odds, one can start to experience mental pressures that come creeping in, the voice of a loved one thousands of miles away, or the creature comforts of home. Therefore, the team intends to document their mental journey as well. At the end of each day, they will discuss their well-being and whether there are any concerns they are feeling.

As they note, they want to have total transparency, as there aren't many people willing to be completely honest and up-front about their mental health—especially when pushed to their limits. This is the time when firefighters traditionally put their walls up and put a brave face on it, which can lead to more profound issues such as depression and PTSD. They hope that their experience and openness will encourage those who need help to speak up.

After the expedition is concluded, the team anticipates that they will have post-expedition depression, so they have wisely prepared counseling and will continue to document their mental well-being. It will take some time to integrate back into normalcy, but they plan on giving a series of speeches and interviews to share their experience.

As I write my final thoughts, I am reminded of the human spirit, this beautiful gift that we are given, and of its strength. Even in our greatest challenges it guides us, it moves us, it unites us, and we embrace it. Our thoughts turn to family, to friends, to our loved ones, and with each step we carry them, and they in turn drive us forward.

I know that these incredibly powerful women will carry this human spirit on their journey. They will succeed in sharing the mental health challenges they endure to help those who suffer from them daily. They will be heroes to young girls and women everywhere who have been told, "You can't do this." And they will carry these weights on their shoulders and call upon them when the hardest of days present themselves.

These women, these firefighters, are our champions, our selfless heroes who put themselves in the harshest environments to better the lives of others. They should be honored as such, supported as such, and afforded the highest status within our communities.

I think now about Georgina carrying her Lego Wonder Woman across Antarctica, but can't help but feel that Nakita, Alison, Beci, Rebecca, Nikki, and Georgina are the real-life Wonder Women, fighting for the justice of equality and raising awareness of mental health and saving lives. They represent the very best of us, and in the simplest of terms, they are ordinary women doing extraordinary things.

Which I think is something we can all get behind.

Inspirational Thoughts from the Antarctic Fire Angels:

Nakita: "Do not feel limited because you are a woman, you are amazing within your own right! We were all ordinary women. We weren't born firefighters, we pushed ourselves, supported others and made our goals reality."

Georgina: "Be the person *you* needed when *you* were growing up. Me? I wanted to be Wonder Woman."

Alison: "Dare to dream and don't be afraid to take on challenges and overcome fears. Perseverance always pays off. Keep pushing and keep practicing until you reach that dream."

Beci: "I want little girls to be inspired to do the jobs or hobbies that traditionally have been seen as male without fear. I want them to believe that nothing is outside of their reach."

Rebecca: "There are no limits to what women and girls can achieve. Don't be afraid of taking a risk."

Nikki: "I want women to be shown that whatever it is they want to achieve, they can tackle it head-on and go for it. What's your Antarctic? This is my Antarctic."

Follow and support the Antarctic Fire Angels on their journey and learn more about training with them:

- Twitter: @Antarctic_Fire
- Instagram: antarcticfireangels
- Facebook: Antarctic Fire Angels
- LinkedIn: Antarctic Fire Angels
- Blog: www.blogsandmusings.com
- GoFundMe: www.gofundme.com/Antarctic-fire-angels

"I'M RUNNING FOR
PRESIDENT BECAUSE THAT'S
WHAT GIRLS DO."

—Elizabeth Warren
Pinky Promise

Chapter Six

~~~~~

The Power
of Leadership

The primary season for the Democratic candidate for president in the 2020 US election gave Americans a chance to look into the mirror and see our reflection.

There were candidates from multiple walks of life and ethnicities among both men and women. We even had our first openly gay candidate; in many ways, it seemed that America had turned a corner and the array of candidates reflected a current time and culture.

As each candidate fought their case on the debate stage and brought to issue the failures and hopes of their communities and country—from healthcare, to equal opportunities, to the environment, to our children's education—it was obvious that many wanted a change and a more inclusive direction.

But with each candidate who dropped out, we saw the field of diversity start to crumble, until finally, when Senator Elizabeth Warren ended her campaign, the death knell sounded for any hope that a woman would win the US presidency in 2020.

This was especially disappointing for many women, given the strong qualifications of the female candidates who had been on the ballot throughout the primary season. By the time I was able to vote in the primaries, Elizabeth Warren was one of the few remaining female candidates and was largely seen by many people, including myself, as one of the most qualified overall.

She had plans for fighting climate change, fixing health care, and ensuring racial and economic justice and opportunity. And these were just three of the eighty (and counting) well-reasoned, detailed plans to improve the lives of millions across the country.[86] Not only was she a champion for change, she also always took time to visit with her supporters, taking selfies with them at the end of her rallies.

On more than one occasion, she spent four hours making sure that everyone who wanted to meet her and have their picture taken with her was able. It was during these after-event moments that people would share their stories, their fears, their struggles, and their gratitude with her. The stories were hard-hitting and heartbreaking, involving struggles with student loan debt, medical bills, and the cost of childcare, among others.[87]

Throughout her campaign, Elizabeth Warren took 100,000 selfies, gave out 100,000 hugs and handshakes, and heard just as many stories.[88] Amid the sound of cameras snapping, she listened and learned of the struggles many were facing in their lives, and for many of these challenges, she could say, "I have a plan for that."

One group that she impacted very deeply were little girls, in the moments when she would kneel down and say, "I am running for president because that is what girls do," interlocking pinkies as a promise so the girls would remember.[89] This was one of her signature gestures throughout her campaign, but it was so much more than a simple gesture—it was an inspiration for so many mothers, grandmothers, and daughters alike.

Attorney Abby K. Wood, like many other mothers during the primary season, took her daughter to see Elizabeth Warren speak at a rally. Afterward, her daughter was able to meet Warren in person. It was one of those magical moments where Warren knelt down to be on the same level as Abby's daughter and made the pinky promise with her. Abby later tweeted about the moment, saying, "On the way home from meeting @ewarren tonight, my daughter—who wore her fanciest cardigan for the occasion—told me, 'Mama, I feel like I met a real president tonight. Like, a real one.'"[90]

The picture that accompanied Abby's tweet perfectly captured the beautiful moment and the essence of Elizabeth Warren—there were many stories like this, but this one would go viral. Abby's tweet gained over a million impressions and 26,000 likes.[91]

As Abby later wrote in her op-ed for NBC News, "The senator told my daughter that running for president should be expected of girls, and they made a pinky promise so she would remember. Setting expectations like this is a crucial aspect of mentorship."[92]

This is what leadership could, should, and *must* look like in America and around the world. Where little girls are able to meet and hear their real-world heroes—women fighting for them, encouraging them, and showing them that there are no limits to what they can achieve.

And that is why it was so disheartening for so many women when another chance to break the barrier that seemed so close had been lost.

In 2016, we had seen Hillary Clinton rise, peak, and fall at the last hurdle, despite winning the popular vote. And now, in 2020, Senators Elizabeth Warren, Kamala Harris (who has since been picked as Joe Biden's running mate), Amy Klobuchar, and Kirsten Gillibrand, Congresswoman Tulsi Gabbard, and author Marianne Williamson had all dropped out of the race because they did not have a path forward to win the Democratic party nomination.

Certainly, Joe Biden's historic choice of Kamala Harris as the first woman of color to be nominated for vice president by a major US political party is something to celebrate. But we must keep pushing forward, so that our heroines are not lost to the history books of defeat but rise to the echelons of greatness where they belong. This is also true for any country that denies or stifles women, especially when they speak up and represent those who do not have a voice or the same freedoms as men.

And women around the world are speaking up, often at great danger and great cost to themselves.

On International Women's Day, March 8, 2020, hundreds of thousands of women across Latin America marched in protest of inequality, femicide, and strict abortion controls.[93] Meanwhile, women's rights activists in Kyrgyzstan who had gathered to march in solidarity against violence were attacked by masked men—and then arrested once the police arrived.[94]

The following day in Mexico, millions of women took part in a day-long strike, called "The Day Without Us." They were protesting the increase in violence against women in Mexico, where it's estimated that ten women are killed *each day*. Moreover, many women are frustrated by what they feel is the government's inaction.[95]

And things are so much worse for women in many conflict-prone and poverty-stricken countries, where they are often forced to live on $1.25 a day to try to meet basic needs while schools, banks, and even hospitals can be hours or days away. Women are also subject to sexual and gender-based violence, which can include abuse from their own family members.[96]

Sadly, the COVID-19 pandemic saw an increase in domestic violence as lockdowns forced many women and children to remain at home—with their abusers.

UN Special Rapporteur on violence against women Dubravka Simonovic said, "For too many women and children, home can be a place of fear and abuse. That situation worsens considerably in cases of isolation such as the lockdowns imposed during the COVID-19 pandemic." And with fewer or no shelters available during lockdowns, risks only increase, including a potential rise in "intimate partner femicides."[97]

This Can Change.
This Must Change.

> "No country can ever truly flourish if it stifles the potential of its women and deprives itself of the contributions of half of its citizens."

— MICHELLE OBAMA

International Women's Day 2020 also brought hope that there's a better way.

Against the backdrop of protests across much of the world, the leaders of Norway, Iceland, Denmark, and Finland showed the world what female leadership looks like. They banded together with the Prime Minister of Sweden to write an opinion piece for CNN expressing their concern about the regression around the world in policies toward women's rights. They emphasized their commitment at the highest level of their governments to achieving gender equality by supporting policies like well-paid, shared parental leave and universal, affordable childcare—policies that help women thrive in the workforce.[98]

It was incredibly refreshing to hear Katrín Jakobsdóttir, the Prime Minister of Iceland, speak about her goal of eliminating the 16 percent pay gap in her country by, in part, becoming the first country to make it illegal for a man to be paid more money than a woman for doing the same job.[99]

For any woman, myself included, who has ever felt the sting of a gender pay gap...or lamented that America still hasn't ratified the Equal Rights Amendment after nearly fifty years...or felt irate that the Paycheck Fairness Act, which would give women equal pay for equal work, has sat in limbo in the Senate for nearly a year at the time of this writing after being passed by the House[100]—I say, how refreshing to see what real leadership committed to women's rights looks like.

And we need more of it *everywhere*.

In their opinion piece, Norway's Prime Minister Erna Solberg, Iceland's Prime Minister Katrín Jakobsdóttir, Denmark's Prime Minister Mette Frederiksen, Finland's Prime Minister Sanna Marin (who became the world's youngest prime minister in 2019), and Sweden's Prime Minister Stefan Löfven also spoke about their commitment to the United Nations Sustainable Development Goals, which are seventeen goals designed to create a better future for everyone.[101]

As the UN says, "In order to leave no one behind, it is important that we achieve them all by 2030."[102]

These goals include no poverty, zero hunger, quality education, clean water, climate action, and gender equality, the latter of which the Nordic leaders stress is the goal "most countries are furthest from reaching."[103]

"World leaders need to intensify their efforts to build a sustainable future where women and girls from all social backgrounds and parts of the world have access to education and health services, have equal opportunities to work and to take part in public life, and are free from the threat of sexual and gender-based violence. On International Women's Day, we, the Nordic Prime Ministers, reaffirm our commitment to this vision. Together, we can do it."[104]

—ERNA SOLBERG, KATRÍN JAKOBSDÓTTIR, METTE FREDERIKSEN, SANNA MARIN, AND STEFAN LÖFVEN

This is what leadership committed to gender equality and women's rights looks like.

And we need more of it *now* if we are to be a well-balanced and inclusive world.

When Elizabeth Warren was on the campaign trail, she said, "I've done pinky promises with babies who are only a couple of weeks old, and I've done pinky promises with elderly women who have been pushed in their wheelchairs by their granddaughters. It's a reminder that for a long time women have been shut out of the process, devalued, told to be quiet. We're just not doing that anymore."[105]

And to her point—I would like to imagine that, with every pinky promise she made, Elizabeth Warren and the other female candidates like her inspired little girls to envision a world where they could easily become president and the kind of leader the world asks for.

A world where girls and women no longer need to fight for equality or basic human rights.

Because their leadership has supported them in every way.

"I've been a proud mentor to many women seeking public office, because I believe we need more women at all levels of government. Women have an equal stake in our future and should have an equal voice in our politics. These are challenging times, but I believe getting more women to run for office is a big part of the solution."

—Kamala Harris

"THE WORST THING
THAT CAN HAPPEN IN A
DEMOCRACY—AS WELL AS
IN AN INDIVIDUAL'S LIFE—
IS TO BECOME CYNICAL
ABOUT THE FUTURE AND
LOSE HOPE: THAT IS THE
END, AND WE CANNOT LET
THAT HAPPEN."

—Hillary Clinton

Chapter Seven

Heidi L. Everett: Civility in Action

On November 8, 2016, millions of women in the United States were poised to celebrate a first Madame President. Not only was the ultimate glass ceiling about to be shattered, but Hillary Clinton's victory would be against a man who was probably the epitome of sexism and abuse.

One of these women was Heidi Everett.

For Heidi, Hillary Clinton was the most qualified person in the history of the United States ever to run for president. Lawyer. Tireless advocate for women and children. First lady. Senator. Secretary of State. And now about to take the greatest seat at the highest table, usually reserved for men. Clinton's campaign poster hung on Heidi's office wall, Clinton's campaign bumper sticker was on her fridge, and Heidi never hesitated to wear Clinton's campaign T-shirt around the ultraconservative Minnesota community in which she lives...even to this day.

Clinton's inclusive message of "Stronger Together" was such a stark contrast to Trump's "Make America

Great Again." For Heidi, "Trump's mocking of those different than him was unacceptable. His mistreatment of women was unacceptable. His bullying was unacceptable. His misuse of power over those less fortunate was unacceptable." That's why "I'm with her" was Heidi's motto.

The election night wasn't just a historic moment for Heidi in the Everett household. It was the first time her three eldest children would be able to cast their votes, and, even though they had felt the "burn" for Bernie Sanders, who was no longer on the ballot, they still felt it was important to get out and vote rather than stay at home.

Throughout the night, Heidi's phone chimed with texts from her children asking meaningful questions about how the process worked, the history of the Electoral College, how maps are drawn up, and the validity of projections based on exit polls and number of precincts reporting. She had raised them well to be inquisitive and involved—especially now, especially that night.

When Ohio was called for Trump, that's when the first real dismay set in for Heidi. Ohio had cast its electoral votes for Barack Obama in 2008 and 2012, and, while Trump had been favored to win the state, no one expected him to win by more than eight points. The Ohio vote had also predicted every US president since 1964.[106]

As more and more results poured in, and Trump edged closer to the magic number of 270 electoral votes needed to win, the great blue Democratic wall that was to hold Trump's advance began to crumble. Heidi's phone chimed with a text from her middle son asking, "What's going on?"

Heidi replied, "I'm having a shot of whiskey and going to bed."

She woke up around two o'clock in the morning to check her phone and saw a news headline with the words *President Trump* in it. She cried herself back to sleep.

Wednesday morning came like a loud knock at the door; the hangover from the shock of Clinton losing had sunk in and left only the prolonged headache of what was to come. The reality is that Heidi didn't have a problem with a Republican candidate winning the election. Throughout our nation's history, the pendulum had swung back and forth between Democrats and Republicans. Heidi had voted for Democrats, Republicans, and Independents across her voting history.

Her problem was with the person "we" elected.

The 2016 election basically told the rest of the world: This is the best we've got. We chose a man as our leader who—up to that point—had mocked disabled people,[107] bragged about grabbing women by their genitals and shoving his tongue in their mouths (claiming it was okay because of his celebrity),[108] reduced women to desirable or undesirable body parts (including his daughter Ivanka) when discussing their value,[109] been accused by many women of varying degrees of sexual assault,[110] and boasted that he could shoot someone in broad daylight on one of the busiest streets in our nation and get away with it.[111]

This is who we as a country held up as the person to represent us.

This is who we as a country held up as the best demonstration of our values and ideals.

This is who we as a country held up in front of our children as an example of how to view and how to treat others.

Many questions swirled through Heidi's mind as she headed off to work that next morning. What was going to happen to our rights? To *Roe v. Wade*, which Trump had promised to overturn?[112] To the future of immigration? To the Supreme Court and courts across the land? To the healthcare that millions relied upon? To the decorum of how we should treat one another?

And, most importantly, what was going to happen to our children's future and our America? The great beacon that shone so brightly in the darkness, calling to so many with these words:

—EMMA LAZARUS, FROM THE POEM "THE NEW COLOSSUS" ON THE STATUE OF LIBERTY

America was now poised to either keep this lamp raised or have the darkness consume it. Only history would tell.

In the weeks that followed, Heidi was simply numb to politics and the reality of who was heading to the White House. Her full-time marketing career and part-time teaching position were welcome distractions. But when the university Women's Center sent an event invite to the Women's March on January 21, 2017, the day after Trump's inauguration, Heidi didn't hesitate to pay the $250 deposit for the eighteen-hour bus trip to Washington, DC.

The bus was packed with women of all ages and backgrounds, but united in one common goal: to speak up and out. Heidi was lucky to sit with a local retiree who knit pussy hats for marchers on the bus as they slowly made their way to the capital. They were tired and a bit cramped from the journey once they arrived, but there was an energy present, as can only be when hundreds of thousands of women come together. It was palpable.

Heidi wanted to march because she refused to simply acquiesce to "Trump being Trump." She refused to be silent.

Her ultimate hope was that Donald Trump would forego his reality-television shenanigans and actually step up and be *presidential*, something that he had joked about but had yet to demonstrate. She wanted him to be that leader, role model, and decent human being that we could only now hope for. She wanted him to surround himself with experts and advisors who could guide him and to actually listen—well, at least for the four years he was to be in office.

When Heidi saw the number of marchers who stood shoulder to shoulder in the streets, green spaces, and hardscapes of Washington, DC, she had such hope. This was so much bigger than a political party—it was the faces of humanity. Mothers and daughters—some carrying their children lofted high on their shoulders—grandmothers and granddaughters walked side by side, holding hands and homemade signs. Couples, sisters, and friends marched with arms intertwined as the crowd slowly moved forward. A sea of pink hats illuminated an otherwise gray Washington day, but the weather did not dampen the spirit of this sisterhood.

Famous musicians, celebrities, activists, and politicians gave rousing speeches. Music filled the air and poetry flowed over the gathered crowd. In cities around the world, millions of women in packed, peaceful gatherings carried signs calling for economic equality, justice, acceptance, respect toward one another, human dignity, and rights for all people. All the things that one should never actually have to ask for, all the things that one should never actually have to march for.

Surely the message would be heard and acted upon. Surely this march could not be ignored.

On the bus ride back home, as the hours waned, Heidi reflected on the day. She felt that they'd accomplished something, that they'd been clear about their hopes and expectations of a president.

That perhaps a future could hold everything they had marched for in its grasp.

That hope quickly faded, however, as with each week and then each month, more and more scandals came to the fore. We endured a daily barrage of narcissistic tweets and misguided policies that plagued the country. There were multiple travel bans targeting refugees and select countries of mostly Muslim faith. There was the firing of acting Attorney General Sally Yates (for refusing to defend Trump's travel ban), of National Security Advisor Michael Flynn (who ended up pleading guilty to lying to the FBI), and of FBI Director James Comey (which Trump later admitted on NBC News was because of "this Russia thing"[113]). The Russia thing, of course, being their interference in our 2016 election.

Trump removed us from the Paris climate deal, accused former President Barack Obama of wiretapping his phones, and endorsed Roy Moore from Alabama to replace Jeff Sessions in the United States Senate, even after Moore had been accused of pursuing sexual relationships with girls as young as fourteen.[114]

And then there was Charlottesville, Virginia. After a day that saw white nationalists and counter-protestors marching and scuffling throughout the city, resulting in the death of one woman, Heather Heyer, Trump would later go on to say there were "some very fine people" on both sides."[115]

And that's just a small portion of how 2017 was shaping up.[116] It didn't take long for "Trump fatigue" to be in full effect. It was unrelenting.

And as 2017 went on, the hope that Heidi had felt after the Women's March was gone.

She explains, "As a mother of three boys, I was just sick about the male behaviors that were being portrayed as acceptable. I couldn't just sit idle or commiserate with others on social media platforms. I couldn't keep talking back to the news broadcasts on the radio in my car. And I couldn't keep avoiding the daily angst by boycotting television and newspapers and media feeds."

Heidi knew she needed to do something more. And, like a record number of women, she decided her "something more" was to run for office.

Up to that point, Heidi's only involvement in politics had been door-knocking for candidates and donating to causes and campaigns. However, she'd always had an interest in it, so much so that when her peers were watching *Miami Vice* and *Cheers* growing up, she could be found watching C-SPAN. It was here that she found larger-than-life heroes she looked up to, including Former US Congresswoman Patricia Schroeder, who represented Colorado from 1973 to 1997. Heidi was delighted when Schroeder became a presidential candidate in 1987 and saddened when she ended her campaign...with tears that did not go unnoticed by the media.[117]

In 2001, Heidi literally ran into Patricia Schroeder at a luncheon as both were snaking their way through the crowded seating. They ended up in a stabilizing embrace, with their hands on each other's upper arms to make sure the other was okay. Heidi was starstruck in a way that she imagined many people are with celebrities, and managed to blurt out, "You've been my hero."

Patricia Schroeder smiled graciously, gave Heidi a reassuring shake, and replied, "Then right now, I'm passing the torch to you."

In 2017, the torch that had been passed on now needed to shine its brightest. It needed to be that "lamp beside the golden door" and bring the soul of America back to what it had once stood for.

Heidi started detailing a potential campaign for a Minnesota State House of Representatives run, which she kicked off one year before the 2018 election.

Unbeknownst to her at the time, thousands of women across the country were also planning their own runs for local, state, and national offices. Much like Heidi, they too had had enough of the daily barrage of negative sentiment and policies. And they too wanted a better role model for their children and the ability to protect so many things they deemed important, like the environment, healthcare, and a woman's right to choose. They wanted the *Handmaid's Tale* to remain a television show and not become a reality.

It can be easy to defend your views behind the veil of social media, but Heidi had to do it on every doorstep she visited and with every phone call she made. She personally made thousands of phone calls and knocked on a few thousand doors. Her inspiring team of volunteers included her father-in-law, a lifelong Republican who felt the party was no longer his Republican party, and her children, niece, and nephew who were new to the process. They put themselves in vulnerable situations where they would knock on a door or make a phone call not knowing if they'd get yelled at, hung up on, or be met with supportive words.

One time, Heidi was confronted while having a beer at a local bar over why Democrats wouldn't approve money for a border wall. She remembers replying that Republicans had controlled the executive and legislative branches of government for more than a year, and if a border wall was important and more than just a campaign sound bite, it could've been done regardless of how Democrats voted.

Heidi knew her run for office would be a challenge, since she lived in a community where her politics didn't align with the majority of voters and where Fox news had a strong grasp on the TV ratings.

In fact, during one League of Women Voters candidate forum, Heidi was the only female candidate on a stage with four older white males. She was the lone voice advocating for women's reproductive healthcare rights and for common-sense gun legislation aimed at protecting women and children in abusive relationships, as well as those with mental illness whose self-inflicted gunshot wounds make up a large number of gun-related deaths each year.

Nevertheless, she persisted.

She purposely chose to run a campaign with the slogan "Civility in Action," because she wanted to help restore civil discourse and moderation in our social and political environment. Unlike Trump's rhetoric of division, Heidi believed that people could always find common ground to build on for the greater good.

As she says, "Too often the various colors and stripes we assign to ourselves divide us."

In one instance of door-knocking, Heidi happened upon an older gentleman having a mild seizure in his garage. He asked her to help him get in a seated position. No other family members were home, although they were expected shortly. Heidi and the gentleman spent about forty-five minutes talking about family, their region, and politics. Although they didn't agree on everything, they had a lot in common. When his family returned home, it was time to leave, so they shook hands.

Then he asked, "Are you pro-life?"

Heidi explained that she wasn't. His final words to her were, "You'll never have my vote, but good luck in the election."

In many ways, this moment was the crux of her campaign. Though we may not agree on every issue, we can choose kindness and civility. We can choose to see past differences and recognize that at the end of the day we're more than members of a political party. We're human beings and what really matters—and what we all share—is our love of family and friends and our hope for the future. These should be the larger clans we seek to identify with, strengthen, and unite.

The Way Forward

> "Among the most striking things that I have
> learned is how much we have in common.
> I've sat down with people everywhere,
> discussing what was in their hearts and on
> their minds. And it doesn't take long to find
> commonality, which is often overlooked,
> ignored, dismissed, and rejected otherwise."
>
> **—HILLARY CLINTON**

While Heidi did not win her race, our story doesn't end
there. At the time of this writing, Trump had just been
acquitted in his impeachment "trial" by a US Senate that
refused to allow witnesses who were willing to come
forward,[118] with damning evidence aplenty pointing to a
president who abused his power and his position, putting
his own interests above those of our nation.[119]

Many Republicans sacrificed their reputations and their
legacies to defend him, which history will reflect upon
for generations to come.

And "Trump fatigue" and fear regarding our rights
and our safety has only intensified since his first year
in office. States around the country have passed laws
challenging a woman's right to choose, and *Roe v. Wade*
is on the ropes.[120] White supremacists have stepped out
of the shadows, and anti-Semitism has raised its ugly

head.[121] We've seen kids in cages at the southern border and families torn apart.[122] There's been a tax cut that benefited the wealthiest Americans and corporations across the country, while our deficit has soared into the trillions.[123] And Trump's 2018 shutdown of the National Security Council's White House pandemic team left us woefully unprepared for the COVID-19 virus pandemic.[124]

Trump has taunted North Korea's Kim Jong Un, calling him "Little Rocket Man,"[125] and ended our nuclear agreement with Iran,[126] two things that may have moved us closer to nuclear proliferation rather than away from it.

And that is why, like Heidi and the thousands of women who ran for office in 2018 and 2020, we must continue to put ourselves on the ballot to make sure our voices are represented.

It's why every election year going forward should be the "Year of the Woman."[127]

It's why the historic nominations of Hillary Clinton for president in 2016 and Kamala Harris for vice president in 2020 must be the first of many more to come.

Women are still nowhere near holding half of elected offices, despite the fact that we make up half the population. Like a listing ship that's taken on water, we'll never be able to truly set sail for a better horizon unless we're equally manned—no pun intended—by men and women. This is true for every country in the world.

> "When I'm sometimes asked, 'When will there be enough women on the Supreme Court?' And I say, 'When there are nine.' People are shocked. But there'd been nine men, and nobody's ever raised a question about that."
>
> **—SUPREME COURT JUSTICE RUTH BADER GINSBURG**

When I reflect upon that "lamp beside the golden door," I am often reminded that the Statue of Liberty stands for hope, justice, enlightenment, and democracy. A beacon that tells of a promised land where freedom and safety have been given to millions of immigrants seeking refuge and opportunity. A symbol of decency, like some great lighthouse that illuminates the darkness, signaling that the journey is almost over, and they will soon be home.

I am also reminded that the Statue of Liberty has been freed from chains that lie at her feet. These represent breaking free from tyranny and servitude,[128] which throughout history has been a woman's story in many ways—a story that can no longer exist in any future, within this country or any other.

In her hand, the Statue of Liberty carries the book of law that governs the land.[129] The book is to represent all peoples, all faiths, and all rights but at this time women, minorities, the LGBTQ community, and immigrants live in fear that their rights will be stripped away or forgotten.

The Statue of Liberty is intended to represent the very best of us: compassion, kindness, and love. That we as a nation should be that bright, enduring democracy shining true as does the north star. That we are a resounding example to the world. That our country, dubbed "the Great Experiment," has been and continues to be a success.

When I reflect on the Trump presidency, I feel that is no longer true under his leadership. I believe Hillary Clinton would have represented us better—that she would have embodied the ideals this great statue represents. I believe our families, education, healthcare, and social programs would have advanced. And instead of words of hate and belittlement, we would have heard words that inspired, lifted, and carried us, much like Heidi's wish for "Civility in Action."

Perhaps former US President Barack Obama said it best. "I'm absolutely confident that, for two years, if every nation on earth was run by women, you would see a significant improvement across the board on just about everything...living standards and outcomes."

And, as all things come full circle, we finish where we started. We vote. We speak up. We speak out. We put ourselves on the ballot.

And we win.

Heidi's Greatest Wish for Girls and Women

I wish for security in many forms.

I wish for girls and women to be secure in access to affordable, quality healthcare in all phases of their lives.

I wish for girls and women to be secure in the knowledge that they are getting equal pay for equal work.

I wish for girls and women to be secure enough to go for a jog or walk the dog without fear of attack.

I wish for girls and women to feel safe in their homes. According to the National Coalition Against Domestic Violence, one in four women experience severe physical or sexual violence by an intimate partner.[130] Home should be a safe place.

Finally, I wish for girls and women to feel secure in themselves: physically, emotionally, intellectually.

"YOUR STORY IS WHAT
YOU HAVE, WHAT YOU
WILL ALWAYS HAVE. IT IS
SOMETHING TO OWN."

—Michelle Obama

It's Time to Tell Your Story

As I look back on the journey of writing this book, it's surreal to think how the world has changed in just a few short months. When I started, America was in the middle of impeachment hearings for a president who, among other things, failed to demonstrate the type of leadership that "we the people" deserve—let alone need.

And now, as I write these words, we are dealing with potentially one of the worst pandemics the world has ever seen. This lack of leadership has led to real and tragic consequences. So far, more than 175,000 people in America have died, and the virus is still spreading.

Doctors and nurses, many of whom are women, have been on the front lines, throwing themselves at this virus, trying to help people breathe again—trying to save lives while risking their own due to a lack of critical personal protective equipment. All the while, watching some of their friends and colleagues succumb to the COVID-19 pandemic.

When the United States had just fifteen cases of the virus, President Trump said this number would be "close to zero" in a couple of days.[131] It wasn't. He also said that the virus would "miraculously" disappear when the weather warmed.[132] It didn't.

And all the while, people were dying, and continued to die.

When governors—including "the woman in Michigan," as he dismissively referred to Gretchen Whitmer—reached out for assistance from the White House, pleading for more ventilators, masks, and help, Trump said, "If they don't treat you right, I don't call."[133]

And all the while, people were dying, and continued to die.

And let us not forget that President Trump shut down the National Security Council's White House pandemic team in 2018, which left us unprotected and unprepared to meet the challenges and demands head-on.[134] In a crisis, it is hard to hide the failures of a government. It is harder to hide the failures of a leader.

And all the while, people will die, and continue to die.

If that wasn't frightening enough, the pandemic left some women even more vulnerable, in lockdown at home with their abusers, or losing their lifeline to education and a better life as schools closed around the world.[135]

It didn't stop there. Even in a pandemic, women's rights continued to be threatened. Texas and Ohio declared abortions elective or nonessential procedures, effectively banning them. And all the while, many women lost their jobs and, in turn, their health insurance and prenatal care as the pandemic continued. Women should not also lose their constitutionally protected right to choose—not now and not ever.[136]

We can do better. We *have to* do better.

Now more than ever, it's so very important that every woman raise her voice and join the ever-growing chorus for women's rights around the world. To strengthen, support, and protect all of us, especially so that those who cannot add their voices due to oppression are represented.

Now more than ever, it's so very important that women's rights are expanded. That we can live in a world where we are safe and free from abuse and inequality, where we can explore any opportunity we choose. Where the words "nontraditional" no longer apply to any careers, and where the rights of women are debated by women in all systems of government.

Now more than ever, we must keep pushing forward to rid the world of patriarchy. We must demand better, inclusive leadership and equal representation for women in all walks of life.

Now more than ever, it is time to stand up and tell *your* story.

It is time to represent all the women who have gone before you and join them in their spirit of getting sh*t done.

If this pandemic has taught us anything, it is that the power of community coming together keeps us strong.

The power of sisterhood has and forever will unite us and move us forward. Together, we do have the power to create a world where *all* women have equal pay, respect, opportunity, and safety.

Every day is ours to own. Every day is ours to give. Every day is an opportunity to change our world.

This is our power.

This is the power of women.

> "You will speak up. You will show up. You will stand up. You will sit in. You will volunteer. You will vote. You will shout out. You will help. You will lend a hand. You will offer your talent and your kindness however you can. And you will radically transform whatever moment you're in."
>
> **—OPRAH WINFREY**

#WomenGetShitDone

#SpeakUpSpeakOut

#NoLongerSilent

Acknowledgments

Throughout my life, I have been surrounded by strong women, and I'd like to think a little bit of that has rubbed off on me. At my highest and lowest points, and every point in between, these women have always been there. They have always inspired me to be my best, often putting the needs of others before their own.

As I reflect on the journey of writing this book, I have been so inspired by each woman I have written about: what they have done, what they continue to do, and through their actions, all those they have benefited. I hope my words do their stories justice. They are the very best of us.

To Dr. Stephanie Bonne, thank you and your colleagues for having the courage to stand up to the NRA and for all that you do to keep us safe from the ongoing epidemic of gun violence. I hope that one day soon, there will be a collaboration with the NRA, and I know you will keep fighting for one until that time. Thank you!

To Patty Turrell, you are an inspiration to so many young girls and women who are a part of the Women's Journey Foundation. It is so encouraging to know that your work is creating a better day, a better life for so many. And that the history of women will not be lost but celebrated for years to come.

To Nakita Ross, Georgina Gilbert, Alison Kibblewhite, Beci Newton, Rebecca Rowe, and Nikki Upton, I am in awe of you, not just because of your Antarctic journey and the many important reasons you're going, but for the bravery you demonstrate every time you put on the uniform of a firefighter. You are and continue to be an inspiration to girls and women everywhere that shows we are strong and powerful. I'm so looking forward to a day of training with you as soon as we can travel again. Thank you for your service, *diolch am eich gwasanaeth.*

To Heidi L. Everett, your grit, determination, and willingness to roll up your sleeves and get sh*t done have been an inspiration to me ever since we met. Your boys and your community at large are so fortunate to have a person of your stature bettering our politics through decency and civility. I'm excited to see what challenge you take on next, as I know the world will be a better place for it.

To the many women in this book who I didn't have a chance to meet, I chose your stories because your work benefits not only your communities, but also the world. And for that, you have my highest praise and profound gratitude. It takes great courage to speak up and out, but it is your strength to act that inspires me most. Thank you.

To Chris McKenney, Brenda Knight, and the entire team at Mango, thank you for everything you've done to bring this book to print in an incredibly challenging year. Brenda, fifteen years ago, you took a chance on an un-agented, un-published writer with a title and a dream. Thank you for all you've done through the years to make my publishing dream come true.

To Andrea Backouris, Hannah DeLis, Mindy Gettier, Jyn Hall, Jane Heber, Jeff Kuns, Frank Mundo, and Jenna Wexler, thank you for reading this book along the way. I feel in many ways we have been on this journey together. Your feedback, support, and words of encouragement were invaluable and kept me going, especially on those blank-page days. I will be forever grateful.

To my mother-in-law, Jane Heber, thank you for all the support this past year. Getting to see you more often has been a highlight and a joy.

To my brother-in-law and sister-in law, Aaron and Hannah DeLis, thank you for always keeping the first booth at Luna open for us with a pot of coffee and the perfect space to write. I know we will all be there together again soon. Cheers to you both!

To my mom, Sally, thank you for instilling in me the determination to fight for others and what, above all, it feels like to be loved unconditionally. You are a mentor, a confidante, and the rock that our family leans on most.

To my dad, Jerry, thank you for always being there. You are the sensibility at the other end of the phone and the best person to get mail from, complete with stickers still attached. After all these years, they mean the world to me, as do you.

To my sister, Mindy, your continued support through the years has no comparison. You let your little sister tag along even when it wasn't cool and even though I had a habit of getting stung by bees or flying off swing sets. You are always a listening ear, and I couldn't have asked for a better sister. Thank you for everything.

To my brother, Gary, who will forever be the most beautiful person I know.

To my husband, my best friend, my writing partner, Jonathan Williams. There's nobody else I'd want to be on this journey of life with. The most beautiful words are always yours.

To all the wonderful women, doing wonderful things within their homes, their communities, their countries, and the world, thank you for getting that sh*t done. And to each and every reader, I hope you enjoyed this journey—that it inspired you, that it moved you, and that you go out there and make amazing sh*t happen! The chorus is calling...

About the Author

Shelly Rachanow is a sought-after writer and speaker for the empowerment of women. Her books have been reviewed or featured in the *Sydney Morning Herald*, *New Zealand Woman's Weekly*, the *Huffington Post*, *Library Journal* (Starred Review), *Sierra* magazine, the *Midwest Book Review*, and *Women's Radio News*, among others. You can always find her writing, drawing, or splitting her time between the US and England, where she loves a good drama on the West End and leaves the cooking to her husband, for the betterment of them both. She is always inspired by the many amazing women she meets who enrich the lives of so many. Follow Shelly at @shellyrachanow on Twitter, @shelly.rachanow on Instagram, and Shelly Rachanow on Facebook.

Endnotes

1   Gulabi Gang, gulabigang.in/what-we-do.php, gulab-igang.in/history.php.

2   Charlotte Alter, Suyin Haynes, and Justin Worland, "TIME 2019 Person of the Year: Greta Thunberg," *TIME*, December 4, 2019, time.com/person-of-the-year-2019-greta-thunberg/.

3   Lily Rothman, "Greta Thunberg Is the Youngest TIME Person of the Year Ever. Here's How She Made History," *TIME*, December 11, 2019, time.com/5746458/youngest-time-person-of-the-year/.

4   Zayed Abdalla, "List of Mass Shootings Since Columbine Massacre," The Villanovan, February 20, 2018, www.villanovan.com/opinion/list-of-mass-shootings-since-columbine-massacre/article_be837bb6-16ae-11e8-b9dc-bfbfd95854b5.html.

5   AFFIRM, affirmresearch.org/affirm-2019-highlights/.

6   AFFIRM, affirmresearch.org/this-is-our-lane/.

7   Bye Bye Plastic Bags, www.byebyeplasticbags.org/team/.

8   Michael Sullivan, "How Teenage Sisters Pushed Bali To Say 'Bye-Bye' To Plastic Bags," *NPR*, January 26, 2019, www.npr.org/sections/goatsandsoda/2019/01/26/688168838/how-teenage-sisters-pushed-bali-to-say-bye-bye-to-plastic-bags.

9   Plastic Oceans International, plasticoceans.org/the-facts/.

10   Sullivan, "How Teenage Sisters Pushed Bali To Say

'Bye-Bye' To Plastic Bags."

11   Melati and Isabel Wijsen, "Our campaign to ban plastic bags in Bali," *TED*, September 2015, www.ted.com/talks/melati_and_isabel_wijsen_our_campaign_to_ban_plastic_bags_in_bali?language=en.

12   Ibid.

13   Ibid.

14   Sullivan, "How Teenage Sisters Pushed Bali To Say 'Bye-Bye' To Plastic Bags."

15   Bye Bye Plastic Bags, www.byebyeplasticbags.org/about/.

16   Wijsen, "Our campaign to ban plastic bags in Bali."

17   "The Story That's Inspired the World," Glamour, May 30, 2013, www.glamourmagazine.co.uk/article/manal-al-sharif-saudi-arabia-story.

18   Jamia Wilson, "Saudi Arabia Was the Last Place in the World to Allow Women to Drive. Manal al-Sharif Helped Change That," Glamour, November 5, 2018, www.glamour.com/story/women-of-the-year-2018-manal-al-sharif.

19   Glamour, "The Story That's Inspired the World."

20   Ibid.

21   Wilson, "Saudi Arabia Was the Last Place in the World to Allow Women to Drive."

22   Glamour, "The Story That's Inspired the World."

23   Manal al-Sharif, "A Saudi woman who dared to drive," TED, June 2013, www.ted.com/talks/manal_al_sharif_a_saudi_woman_who_dared_to_drive?language=en.

24   Glamour, "The Story That's Inspired the World."

25   Wilson, "Saudi Arabia Was the Last Place in the World to Allow Women to Drive."

26   Lulu Garcia Navarro, "TRANSCRIPT: Saudi Women Activists Again in Court to Fight for Right to Drive," NPR Weekend Edition Sunday, March 8, 2020, www. npr.org/2020/03/08/813384331/saudi-women-activ-ist-to-return-to-court-to-fight-for-right-to-drive.

27   Press Release, "Announcing Manal al-Sharif's Free-dom Drive Campaign," Human Rights Foundation, March 19, 2019, hrf.org/press_posts/announcing-manal-al-sharifs-freedom-drive-campaign/.

28   Wilson, "Saudi Arabia Was the Last Place in the World to Allow Women to Drive."

29   Melissa Healy, "Suicide rates for US teens and young adults are the highest on record," Los Angeles Times, June 18, 2019, www.latimes.com/science/la-sci-suicide-rates-rising-teens-young-adults-20190618-story.html.

30   Jessica Valenti, "Worldwide sexism increases suicide risk in young women," The Guardian, May 28, 2015, www.theguardian.com/commentisfree/2015/may/28/worldwide-sexism-increases-suicide-risk-in-young-women.

31   "The Dove Self-Esteem Project: Our Mission in Action," Dove, November 1, 2016, www.dove.com/us/en/dove-self-esteem-project/our-mission/the-dove-self-esteem-project-our-mission-in-action.html.

32   Women's Journey Foundation, "Video: The Girls Self Esteem Conference featuring Darby Walker, present-ed by the Women's Journey Foundation," October 31,

2016, womensjourneyfoundation.org/girls-program/.

33 Maya Salam, "Women's History Myths, Debunked," The New York Times, March 1, 2019, www.nytimes. com/2019/03/01/us/womens-history-month-myths. html.

34 The Editors of Encyclopaedia Britannica, "Mary Ann Bickerdyke," Britannica, www.britannica.com/biogra-phy/Mary-Ann-Bickerdyke.

35 Margot Lee Shetterly, "Katherine Johnson Biogra-phy," Nasa, Updated February 24, 2020, www.nasa. gov/content/katherine-johnson-biography.

36 Ibid.

37 Ibid.

38 Ibid.

39 Debra Michals, "Alice Paul," National Women's History Museum, www.womenshistory.org/educa-tion-resources/biographies/alice-paul.

40 Ibid.

41 Ibid.

42 Alice Paul Institute, www.alicepaul.org/who-was-alice-paul/.

43 Veronica Stracqualursi, "Virginia reaches long-awaited milestone by ratifying Equal Rights Amendment, but legal fight looms," CNN, January 27, 2020, www.cnn.com/2020/01/27/politics/virgin-ia-equal-rights-amendment-trnd/index.html.

44 Rep. Carolyn B. Maloney, "Women's Museum Bill Sponsors Celebrate House Passage," Press Release, February 11, 2020, maloney.house.gov/media-center/press-releases/women-s-museum-bill-sponsors-cel-

ebrate-house-passage.

45   Ibid.

46   Women's Journey Foundation, womensjourney-
foundation.org/girls-program/.

47   Lauren Breedlove, "The Uplifting Ways Italians
Are Coping with the Coronavirus Lockdown," Afar,
March 16, 2020, www.afar.com/magazine/ital-
ians-cope-with-coronavirus-lockdown-with-uplift-
ing-messages.

48   Sara Spary and Sharon Braithwaite, "Confined
to their homes, Italian neighbors sing together
to boost morale," CNN, March 13, 2020, www.cnn.
com/2020/03/13/europe/italian-neighbors-sing-sc-
li-intl/index.html.

49   Breedlove, "The Uplifting Ways Italians Are Coping."

50   Breedlove, "The Uplifting Ways Italians Are Coping."

51   Matthew Dessem, "Europeans Under Lockdown Are
Singing Together and Giving Their Health Care Workers Citywide Ovations," Slate, March 14, 2020, slate.
com/culture/2020/03/coronavirus-quarantine-sin-
galong-ovation-applause-italy-spain-bella-ciao-vo-
lare-nessun-dorma-verbena.html.

52   "Clap for Carers: UK in 'emotional' tribute to NHS
and care workers," BBC News, March 27, 2020, www.
bbc.com/news/uk-52058013.

53   "Coronavirus: Thousands volunteer to help NHS
with vulnerable," BBC News, March 25, 2020, www.
bbc.com/news/uk-52029877.

54   Alaa Elassar, "Two siblings held a porch concert
for a neighbor who is self-isolating," CNN, March 17,
2020, www.cnn.com/2020/03/17/us/children-per-

form-coronavirus-elderly-neighbor-self-isola-
tion-trnd/index.html.

55   Sharyn Alfonsi, "Early Results From 174 Flint Chil-
      dren Exposed to Lead During Water Crisis Shows
      80% of Them Will Require Special Education
      Services," 60 Minutes, March 15, 2020, www.cbsnews.
      com/news/flint-water-crisis-effect-on-children-60-
      minutes-2020-03-15/.

56   Mari Copeny, www.maricopeny.com/about.

57   Ibid.

58   Alfonsi, "Early Results From 174 Flint Children Ex-
      posed to Lead During Water Crisis."

59   Ibid.

60   Ibid.

61   Ibid.

62   The Obama Foundation, www.obama.org/girlsop-
      portunityalliance/take-action/get-the-facts/.

63   Ibid.

64   Ibid.

65   Ibid.

66   Ibid.

67   Ibid.

68   Ibid.

69   Study Hall Educational Foundation, www.studyhall-
      foundation.org/about_shef.php.

70   Study Hall Educational Foundation, www.studyhall-
      foundation.org/prerna-girls/index.php.

71   Ibid.

72   Ibid.

73   Study Hall Educational Foundation, www.studyhall-foundation.org/prerna-boys/index.php.

74   YouTube Originals, "Why 98 Million Adolescent Girls Aren't in School #CreatorsForChange," YouTube, March 17, 2020, www.youtube.com/watch?v=HzOPah2JzJE.

75   "'Ice Maiden' team celebrates Antarctica ski record," BBC News, January 21, 2018, www.bbc.com/news/uk-42759027.

76   Rachel Dale, Jack Royston, Alex Diaz, "Croydon tram crash survivors tell of horrific scenes as it emerges vehicle rolled THREE TIMES," The Sun, November 9, 2016, Updated November 10, 2016, www.thesun.co.uk/news/2153148/croydon-tram-crash-survivor-tells-of-carnage-after-passenger-decapitated-beside-him-and-others-left-trapped-and-screaming-in-the-wreckage/.

77   Dale, et al. "Croydon tram crash."

78   Visual Journalism team, "Grenfell Tower: What happened," BBC News, October 29, 2019, www.bbc.com/news/uk-40301289.

79   "'People were waiting to die': London fire witnesses speak – video," The Guardian, June 14, 2017, www.theguardian.com/uk-news/video/2017/jun/14/like-something-out-of-a-horror-movie-london-fire-witnesses-speak-video.

80   "Grenfell Tower: What happened."

81   "Post-traumatic stress disorder (PTSD)," Mayo Clinic, www.mayoclinic.org/diseases-conditions/post-traumatic-stress-disorder/symptoms-causes/syc-20355967.

82   The Fire Fighters Charity, www.firefighterscharity.
      org.uk/.

83   The Fawcett Society, www.fawcettsociety.org.uk/
      about.

84   The Fawcett Society, www.fawcettsociety.org.uk/
      about.

85   The Harlequins Foundation, www.harlequins.foun-
      dation/about-us/.

86   Elizabeth Warren, elizabethwarren.com/plans.

87   Rebecca Jennings, "Why selfie lines are crucial to
      Elizabeth Warren's campaign," Vox, December 20,
      2019, www.vox.com/the-goods/2019/9/19/20872718/
      elizabeth-warren-2020-selfie-line.

88   Ibid.

89   Aris Folley, "Viral photo shows Elizabeth Warren
      doing 'pinky promise' with young girl," The Hill, Au-
      gust 3, 2019, thehill.com/blogs/blog-briefing-room/
      news/456077-viral-photo-shows-elizabeth-warren-
      doing-pinky-promise-with.

90   Abby K. Wood, "Elizabeth Warren's selfie with my
      daughter went viral because pinkie promises mean
      something," NBC News, September 18, 2019, www.
      nbcnews.com/think/opinion/elizabeth-warren-s-sel-
      fie-my-daughter-went-viral-because-pinkie-nc-
      na1055561.

91   Ibid.

92   Ibid.

93   Natalia A. Ramos Miranda and Daina Beth Solo-
      mon, "Huge turnout, some violence at Latin America
      Women's Day marches," Reuters, March 7, 2020,

www.reuters.com/article/us-womens-day-latina-merica/huge-turnout-some-violence-at-latin-america-womens-day-marches-idUSKBN20V06X.

94   Olga Dzyubenko and Vladimir Pirogov, "Women's rights activists attacked then detained in Kyrgyzstan," Reuters, March 8, 2020, www.reuters.com/article/us-womens-day-kyrgyzstan-protests/womens-rights-activists-attacked-then-detained-in-kyrgyzstan-idUSKBN20V0GT.

95   "Mexican women strike to protest against gender-based violence," BBC News, March 9, 2020, www.bbc.com/news/world-latin-america-51811040.

96   Women for Women International, www.womenforwomen.org/why-women.

97   Radina Gigova, "Domestic violence 'very likely' to increase during lockdowns, UN warns," CNN, March 28, 2020, edition.cnn.com/world/live-news/coronavirus-outbreak-03-28-20-intl-hnk/h_553decc4c49f2aaeba0498d0520d74b7.

98   Erna Solberg, Katrín Jakobsdóttir, Mette Frederiksen, Sanna Marin and Stefan Löfven, "Nordic Prime Ministers: We are committed to protecting women's rights," CNN, March 6, 2020, www.cnn.com/2020/03/06/opinions/international-womens-day-solberg-jakobsdttir-frederiksen-marin-lfven/index.html.

99   Ibid.

100   Toni Van Pelt, "The Paycheck Fairness Act Would Help Close the Gender Wage Gap. Why Won't the Senate Pass It?" Fortune, August 26, 2019, fortune.com/2019/08/26/womens-equality-day-paycheck-fairness-act/.

101 Solberg, Jakobsdóttir, et al, "Nordic Prime Ministers."

102 United Nations, www.un.org/sustainabledevelopment/sustainable-development-goals/.

103 Solberg, Jakobsdóttir, et al, "Nordic Prime Ministers."

104 Ibid.

105 Adam Carlson, "The Real Story Behind Elizabeth Warren's Viral Pinky Promises with Girls as She Champions 'Big Change' for America," People, October 18, 2019, people.com/politics/elizabeth-warren-2020-pinky-promises-with-young-girls/.

106 Ciara McCarthy and Claire Phipps, "Election results timeline: how the night unfolded," The Guardian, November 9, 2016, www.theguardian.com/us-news/2016/nov/08/presidential-election-updates-trump-clinton-news.

107 Daniel Arkin, "Donald Trump Criticized After He Appears to Mock Reporter Serge Kovaleski," NBC News, November 26, 2015, www.nbcnews.com/politics/2016-election/donald-trump-criticized-after-he-appears-mock-reporter-serge-kovaleski-n470016.

108 Scott Neuman, "Billy Bush: 'Of Course' It's Trump's Voice On 'Access Hollywood' Tape," NPR, December 4, 2017, www.npr.org/sections/thetwo-way/2017/12/04/568255700/billy-bush-of-course-its-trumps-voice-on-access-hollywood-tape.

109 Louis Nelson, "Trump told Howard Stern it's OK to Call Ivanka a 'piece of a—,'" POLITICO, October 8, 2016, www.politico.com/story/2016/10/trump-ivan-

ka-piece-of-ass-howard-stern-229376.

110   Meghan Keneally, "List of Trump's accusers and their allegations of sexual misconduct," ABC News, June 25, 2019, abcnews.go.com/Politics/list-trumps-accusers-allegations-sexual-misconduct/story?id=51956410.

111   Lauren Aratani, "Trump couldn't be prosecuted if he shot someone on Fifth Avenue, lawyer claims," The Guardian, October 23, 2019, www.theguardian.com/us-news/2019/oct/23/donald-trump-immune-shoot-fifth-avenue-murder.

112   Dan Mangan, "Trump: I'll appoint Supreme Court justices to overturn Roe v. Wade abortion case," CNBC, October 19, 2016, www.cnbc.com/2016/10/19/trump-ill-appoint-supreme-court-justices-to-overturn-roe-v-wade-abortion-case.html.

113   Tucker Higgins, "President Trump contradicts himself by claiming he didn't fire James Comey over the Russia probe," CNBC, May 31, 2018, www.cnbc.com/2018/05/31/president-trump-contradicts-himself-by-claiming-he-didnt-fire-james-comey-over-the-russia-probe.html.

114   Stephanie McCrummen, Beth Reinhard and Alice Crites, "Woman says Roy Moore initiated sexual encounter when she was 14, he was 32," The Washington Post, November 9, 2017, www.washingtonpost.com/investigations/woman-says-roy-moore-initiated-sexual-encounter-when-she-was-14-he-was-32/2017/11/09/1f495878-c293-11e7-afe9-4f60b5a-6c4a0_story.html.

115   Rosie Gray, "Trump Defends White-Nationalist Protesters: 'Some Very Fine People on Both Sides,'"

The Atlantic, August 15, 2017, www.theatlantic.com/
politics/archive/2017/08/trump-defends-white-
nationalist-protesters-some-very-fine-people-on-
both-sides/537012/.

116   Ryan Teague Beckwith, "The Year in Trump: Mem-
orable Moments from the President's First Year in
Office," TIME, January 11, 2018, time.com/5097411/
donald-trump-first-year-office-timeline/.

117   Elise Hu, "Campaign Trail Tears: The Changing
Politics of Crying," NPR, November 25, 2011, www.npr.
org/2011/11/25/142599676/campaign-trail-tears-the-
changing-politics-of-crying.

118   Jeremy Herb, Kylie Atwood and Manu Raju, "John
Bolton says he is prepared to testify in Senate trial
if subpoenaed," CNN, January 6, 2020, www.cnn.
com/2020/01/06/politics/john-bolton-testify-im-
peachment-subpoena/index.html.

119   Salvador Hernandez, "Here's the Most Important
Evidence from the Trump Impeachment Trial," Buzz-
Feed News, January 30, 2020, www.buzzfeednews.
com/article/salvadorhernandez/impeachment-tri-
al-trump-evidence-summary.

120   Planned Parenthood, www.plannedparenthoo-
daction.org/issues/abortion.

121   Jennifer Calfas, "White Supremacists Amp Up
Propaganda, Report Says," The Wall Street Journal, February 12, 2020, www.wsj.com/articles/
white-supremacists-amp-up-propaganda-re-
port-says-11581536690.

122   Clara Long, "Written Testimony: 'Kids in Cages:
Inhumane Treatment at the Border,'" Human Rights
Watch, July 11, 2019, www.hrw.org/news/2019/07/11/

written-testimony-kids-cages-inhumane-treatment-border#.

123   Shane Croucher, "Trump's 2017 Tax Cuts Helped Super-Rich Pay Lower Rate Than Bottom 50 Percent: Economists," Newsweek, October 9, 2019, www.newsweek.com/trump-tax-cuts-jobs-act-wealth-economists-inequality-1464048.

124   Laurie Garrett, "Trump Has Sabotaged America's Coronavirus Response," Foreign Policy, January 31, 2020, foreignpolicy.com/2020/01/31/coronavirus-china-trump-united-states-public-health-emergency-response/.

125   Meghan Keneally, "From 'fire and fury' to 'rocket man,' the various barbs traded between Trump and Kim Jong Un," ABC News, June 11, 2018, abcnews.go.com/International/fire-fury-rocket-man-barbs-traded-trump-kim/story?id=53634996.

126   Mark Landler, "Trump Abandons Iran Nuclear Deal He Long Scorned," The New York Times, May 8, 2018, www.nytimes.com/2018/05/08/world/middleeast/trump-iran-nuclear-deal.html.

127   Elaine Kamarck, "2018: Another 'Year of the Woman,'" The Brookings Institution, November 7, 2018, www.brookings.edu/blog/fixgov/2018/11/07/2018-another-year-of-the-woman/.

128   National Park Service, www.nps.gov/stli/learn/historyculture/abolition.htm.

129   National Park Service, www.nps.gov/stli/upload/STLI-Statue-Stats_Rev.pdf.

130   National Coalition Against Domestic Violence, ncadv.org/statistics.

131   Steve Benen, "A line on the coronavirus outbreak Trump may come to regret," *MSNBC*, February 28, 2020, www.msnbc.com/rachel-maddow-show/line-coronavirus-outbreak-trump-may-come-re-gret-n1144686.

132   Bess Levin, "Trump Claims Coronavirus Will 'Miraculously' Go Away by April," *Vanity Fair*, February 11, 2020, www.vanityfair.com/news/2020/02/donald-trump-coronavirus-warm-weather.

133   Matt Perez, "Trump Encourages Pence to Ignore Democratic Governors: 'If They Don't Treat You Right, I Don't Call,'" Forbes, March 27, 2020, www.forbes.com/sites/mattperez/2020/03/27/trump-encourages-pence-to-ignore-democratic-governors-if-they-dont-treat-you-right-i-dont-call/#6023d12c5a45.

134   Laurie Garrett, "Trump Has Sabotaged America's Coronavirus Response," Foreign Policy, January 31, 2020, foreignpolicy.com/2020/01/31/coronavirus-china-trump-united-states-public-health-emergency-response/.

135   Radina Gigova, "Domestic violence 'very likely' to increase during lockdowns, UN warns," CNN, March 28, 2020, edition.cnn.com/world/live-news/coronavirus-outbreak-03-28-20-intl-hnk/h_553decc4c49f2aaeba0498d0520d74b7.

136   Amy Braunschweiger, "Ohio, Texas Use COVID-19 to Stop Abortions," Human Rights Watch, March 24, 2020, www.hrw.org/news/2020/03/24/ohio-texas-use-covid-19-stop-abortions#.

Mango Publishing, established in 2014, publishes an eclectic list of books by diverse authors—both new and established voices—on topics ranging from business, personal growth, women's empowerment, LGBTQ studies, health, and spirituality to history, popular culture, time management, decluttering, lifestyle, mental wellness, aging, and sustainable living. We were recently named 2019 *and* 2020's #1 fastest growing independent publisher by *Publishers Weekly*. Our success is driven by our main goal, which is to publish high quality books that will entertain readers as well as make a positive difference in their lives.

Our readers are our most important resource; we value your input, suggestions, and ideas. We'd love to hear from you—after all, we are publishing books for you!

Please stay in touch with us and follow us at:

Facebook: Mango Publishing

Twitter: @MangoPublishing

Instagram: @MangoPublishing

LinkedIn: Mango Publishing

Pinterest: Mango Publishing

Newsletter: mangopublishinggroup.com/newsletter

Join us on Mango's journey to reinvent publishing, one book at a time.